Simple Jewelry

Simple Jewelry

R W Stevens

Studio Vista London

Watson-Guptill Publications New York

General Editor Jean Richardson
© R. W. Stevens 1966
Published in London by Studio Vista Limited
Blue Star House, Highgate Hill, London N19
and in New York by Watson-Guptill Publications
165 West 46th Street, New York 10036
Library of Congress Catalog Card Number 67-10434
Set in Folio Grotesque 8 and 9 pt.
Printed in the Netherlands
by N.V. Grafische Industrie Haarlem

Contents

Introduction

Many people look upon jewelry as a mystery craft requiring special skill, expensive materials and tools etc., but this is a misconception in many ways. Certainly a good percentage of the fine jewelry seen in shops is of a complex nature, requiring specialist skill and equipment, but there remains a vast field of simpler jewelry which is suitable for the beginner to make.

It is the intention of this book, therefore, to make jewelry - a craft which is usually left to the professional - a more accessible craft, a way by which you can create your own individual jewelry to suit you and your friends. The pieces are so designed and selected that, with a minimum of tools, a range of attractive articles of jewelry can be simply made and confidence gained in the beginnings of craftsmanship.

It is necessary, when beginning any craft, to give instruction which is limited to particular examples and provides a step-by-step procedure which is easy to follow. This is the case in the following exercises, and if they are properly followed, they will provide certain experience in the workings of materials which, once gained, will prove a satisfying basis for the reader to experiment further. There are always many varieties to the examples and methods given, and it is this that makes the experiment worthwhile, for in this way a piece of jewelry becomes more individual and worth the effort to its creator.

1 General information

Tools

The production and the types of jewelry included in this book have been carefully planned to avoid the usual expensive list of tools and workshop facilities. Instead, only the minimum of tools is needed, and these will justify their cost throughout the exercises and also in household jobs.

The progressive planning of the following chapters allows the reader to begin with very little outlay and to increase the number of tools required gradually as confidence is gained and the pieces become slightly more complex.

The tools required for each set of articles are listed at the beginning of each chapter and are readily available from local suppliers, but if any difficulty is experienced the list of retailers on p. 95 should be consulted.

Materials

The workable properties of metals vary a great deal, and each is suited to certain jobs. For the jewelry-making in this book, it is best to have a reasonably soft metal, one which is easy to bend and to cut and which is inexpensive. Two metals satisfy these requirements. These are copper and silver. Silver, of course, is a precious metal and therefore more expensive than copper. However, it is not as highly priced as many people think, and no one piece of jewelry from this book made in silver will prove expensive. It is suggested, therefore, that copper be generally used, and that once confidence is gained the reader will like to make an occasional piece in silver.

Both copper and silver can be bought in wire and sheet forms, and are easily obtainable. The suppliers of silver are listed in the back of this book, together with the larger suppliers of copper, though in the case of the latter, local shops may well have what is required. Plumbers shops, for instance, often stock copper wire of the size needed.

The actual sizes and quantities of metal required are given at the beginning of each exercise, but it is best to buy enough for several pieces in order to save needless travelling or postage. This can be easily estimated by taking the total of the amounts given.

The finishing of articles

As the materials will usually be already polished when purchased, the real secret of a good final finish is to take great care not to mark the surfaces unnecessarily whilst working. If any bad marks do occur, these must be removed before polishing, and this is done by using a very fine grade of wet and dry emery paper. The correct grade to use is 320. If coarser is used, the surface will become too badly scratched to be polished. To use, tear or cut the sheet into convenient strips or pieces, dip it into water and carefully rub the marked areas until the marks disappear, then wash the article clean before polishing.

Polishing

The polishing of the small intricate shapes that occur in jewelry is best carried out at home by the hand method of brushing with a soft brass brush. This type of small hand brush has fine brass bristles and can be obtained at tool shops or shoe repairers who sell them for cleaning suede.

The actual brushing is simply done, using a fairly strong solution of soap and water as a lubricant. Just dip the brush into the soapy water and brush the article till bright. Finally wash it in clean water to remove the soap and dry on a soft rag. To obtain the most satisfactory finish, it is advisable to keep the strokes of the brush running one way over the jewelry, so giving a more uniform polish.

Lacquering

Once the article is polished satisfactorily, it is relatively easy to retain the brightness by occasional repolishing. However, one way of avoiding tarnishing completely is to lacquer the surfaces. This stops the air getting to them. It is easily done by buying a bottle of clear lacquer of the cellulose type, or clear nail varnish, and carefully painting the surface evenly with a small soft brush. Make sure that the lacquer is absolutely dry before handling the surfaces, otherwise they will be spoilt. If they do become damaged, use a cellulose thinner to remove the old lacquer completely, then repolish and re-lacquer.

Plating

If you so desire, copper jewelry can be silver or gold plated. Most towns have platers who will do this job quite cheaply and this will give added quality to the pieces chosen.

It must be remembered, however, that plating is liable to wear and must not be cleaned with a brass brush or metal polish, both of which would be too coarse. Plated articles should be cleaned with a soft hair brush used with soapy water, then dried carefully with a soft duster.

2 Bending wire forms

As an introduction to the craft of jewelry, the simple action of wire bending affords the most satisfactory first step. Only very few tools are required, and the materials are inexpensive and readily available. The production methods used in this chapter are based on commonsense and are very straightforward.

A place to work

Any steady table or working area of approximately 3′ by 2′ will suffice, although it is not advisable to use a polished table top because in later exercises heat from soldering may damage the surface. A piece of hardboard laid on your working area will provide a good surface to work on and will save worry over possible cuts and scratches etc.

Materials

The round section copper or silver wire used throughout the following series of exercises should be slightly under 1/16″ in diameter. Wire is usually sold in a range of sizes called Imperial Standard Wire Gauge in Great Britain or Band S gauge in the U.S.A., and it will help to know when buying that you require 16 or 17 gauge. This thickness of wire allows easy working plus a certain rigidity in the finished piece of jewelry. Try to avoid rolling the wire into a tight coil, because any unnecessary bends will have to be removed before use.

Tools required

Three pairs of pliers are the only tools required for the articles to be made in this chapter. These are the small jewelry type of pliers and are readily available at tool shops, but make certain when buying them that the inside of the jaws are smooth and do not have a rough grip surface. (See Figs. 1, 2 and 3.)

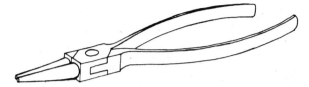

Fig. 1 Round nosed

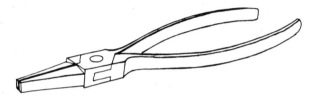

Fig. 2 Flat nosed

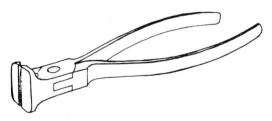

Fig. 3 End cutters

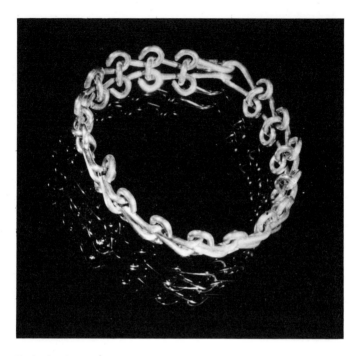

Bracelet

This bracelet is designed to fit the average adult wrist. However, because it is made from wire and is therefore light in weight and delicate in appearance, it is also a most suitable bracelet to be worn by a child.

It is very easy to adjust the length of the bracelet to fit any size wrist when joining the actual links together. This is done simply by not using as many of the links as stated for a smaller wrist, or by adding one or two more so that it fits a larger one.

If this bracelet is intended for a child, do remember that it is especially important that all sharp edges are removed so that it does not scratch.

Length of wire required: 36½".

To begin this bracelet, use the end cutters to cut seventeen 2" lengths of wire. Then straighten them between your fingers.

Take one of the wires firmly between finger and thumb and grasp one end in the widest part of the tapered jaws of the round pliers (Fig. 4).

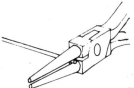

Fig. 4

Bend the end back towards the main body of the wire, until it is about 1/16" away, so making an open loop (Fig. 5).

Fig. 5

Do the same to the other end, being careful to bend the second loop so that it is in line with the first (Fig. 6). If the loops tend to be out of line, hold one of them in the round pliers and, with the flat pliers, twist the other loop until right.

Fig. 6

Having satisfactorily reached this stage, bend all other wires in the same way.

Next, taking one of the wires, hold it centrally in the widest part of the round jawed pliers so that the loops, equally spaced from the jaws, are vertical and topmost (Fig. 7).

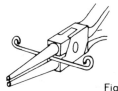

Fig. 7

Placing a finger at one end and a thumb at the other, push the two ends downwards round the lower jaw of the pliers until the two loops meet back to back (Fig. 8).

Bring all the wire units to the same stage.

The last step before assembly is the curving of each link so

Fig. 8

Fig. 9

Fig. 10

Fig. 11

Fig. 12

that the bracelet will form round the wrist correctly.

This is carried out with each link in turn by holding the end of the central loop horizontally between the jaws of the round pliers (Fig. 9). Then press the free part of the link downwards with your thumb, so bending the link until the front part is curved at right angles (Fig. 10).

To assemble the links, hold one link horizontally, then place a second at right angles to the underside of the first, so that the long centre loop of the second slips through the centre loop of the first (Fig. 11). Push through and then twist the second link into the same position as the first, making certain that it fits into the open loops (Fig. 12).

Fit all the links together in the same way to produce the length of chain required. This should only be long enough to go round the wrist, so allow for the extra length of the catch which will make the slight looseness finally required. If too long or too short, adjust as previously described.

When laid round the wrist, the bracelet should form to the shape easily. If this does not happen, then gently bend the assembled chain into a tighter circle so that movement of the links is increased.

To make the catch for this bracelet, cut a 2½" length of wire and straighten it with your fingers. Find the middle and holding this point in the wide part of the jaws of the round pliers (Fig. 13), bend with finger and thumb into a 'U' with both sides equal (Fig. 14).

This done, with the flat pliers find half-way down each side and make a slight bend outwards (Fig. 15). Next, hold the bottom curve of the U in the wide part of the round pliers (Fig. 16), and with finger and thumb squeeze the two ends together until the side arms meet (Fig. 17).

If the two ends are unequal, cut a little off the longest arm until they are the same length.

With the round pliers, bend the two ends downwards into a quarter circle and bend the ends of the long loop in the same way (Fig. 18). Finally, with the middle of the jaws of the round pliers, hold the catch just before the curved ends of the wire so that the ends are just showing through (Fig. 19). Bend upwards and back until the first curve is about 1/16″ away from the main body of the catch (Fig. 20).

The catch, now complete, should be threaded on to the first link of the bracelet. This is done by holding it lengthways against the two open loops of the link, and hooking it over the left-hand one (Fig. 21). Then, pulling the catch towards you, push it over the other open loop (Fig. 22). Lastly, twist the catch into its proper position (Fig. 23).

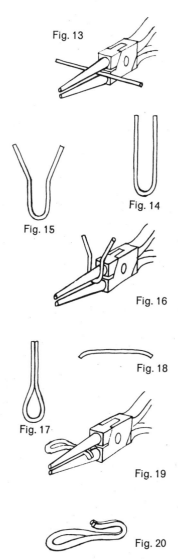

Fig. 13

Fig. 14

Fig. 15

Fig. 16

Fig. 17

Fig. 18

Fig. 19

Fig. 20

15

Fig. 21

Fig. 22

To complete the bracelet, all open links should now be closed to form a stronger union. This is done by carefully squeezing each loop in turn with flat pliers. From the back insert one of the jaws of the pliers between the two open loops, and the other on the outer edge of the loop. Then, holding the link firmly to avoid any twisting, gently squeeze the loop until the gap closes (Fig. 24).

The final finishing and polishing of the bracelet should now be carried out. Special care should be taken to remove with wet and dry paper any sharp burrs at the end of the catch, for these may damage clothes. If unnecessary plier marks have been avoided, only the removal of these burrs and polishing will be required.

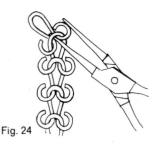

Fig. 23

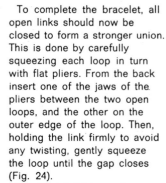

Fig. 24

Necklace

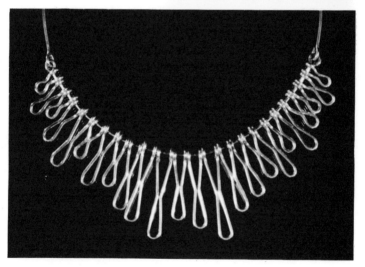

The following instructions are intended to produce a necklace to fit an average-sized neck and to hang in a fairly high position. If you wish to change either of these factors, it is only necessary to adjust the length of the two long connecting side wires accordingly. This is easily done in the final stages.

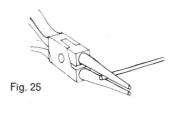

Fig. 25

Fig. 26

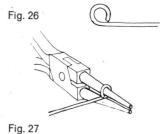

Fig. 27

Fig. 28

Fig. 29

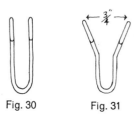

Fig. 30   Fig. 31

Length of wire required: 7'6".

Cut 24 pieces of wire in random lengths varying between 2" and 4". Straighten with the fingers.

Grasping the very end of one of the wires in the middle of the jaws of the round pliers (Fig. 25), bend the end back towards the main body of the wire until it touches, so making a loop (Fig. 26).

Next, holding the loop in the pliers so that one of the round jaws is under the joint (Fig. 27), bend the loop downwards until the axis is centralised (Fig. 28).

Make a similar loop at the other end of the wire, keeping it in line with the first and the joins on the same side.

Having satisfactorily carried this out, do the same to all the remaining lengths of wire.

Taking one of the looped wires, find the middle and hold it in the thickest part of the jaws of the round nosed pliers, so that the two loops are horizontal to the jaws (Fig. 29). Then, placing a finger at one end and a thumb on the other, push the wire into a U shape, so that the two loops are equal from the bend (Fig. 30).

Halfway along the length of each side, bend outwards until the ends are $\frac{3}{4}"$ apart (Fig. 31). If you find difficulty in holding the smaller pieces, hold one of the arms with pliers while bending the other.

Next, hold the bottom of the

U in the thickest part of the jaws of the round pliers, then squeeze the two ends towards each other with finger and thumb (Fig. 32).

Finally, using flat pliers, slightly bend each of the loops at the top of the unit until they are parallel (Fig. 33). Finish all the wire units to the same stage.

When done, the next stage is to make the connecting wire which is to hold the units round the neck. This is made by cutting a 7″ length of wire and straightening it. Then, holding one end in the widest part of the jaws of the round pliers, put a loop at one end similar to those on the small units (Fig. 34).

Now thread the units on to this wire (Fig. 35). Arrange them to your liking, keeping the majority of the longest ones towards the centre. (See photograph of complete necklace.) When it looks satisfactory, put a loop in line with the first at the other end of the wire, so that the units are contained between them (Fig. 36). The units should be held close together but loose enough to swing freely. If too tight or too loose, ease the arms of the units apart or together with flat pliers until correctly spaced.

When hanging properly, gently bend the wire spine between your fingers to the correct curve for the neck.

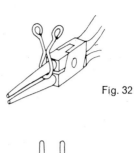

Fig. 32

Fig. 33

Fig. 34

Fig. 35

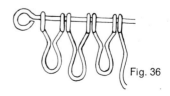

Fig. 36

Fig. 37

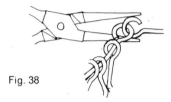

Fig. 38

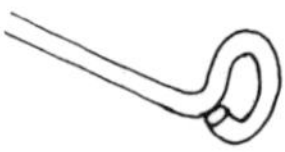

Fig. 39

Fig. 40

Fig. 41

Fig. 42

Make sure that the loops at each end lie flat when round neck.

For the two wires that go round the neck, cut two pieces 6¼" long, straighten and make a loop in one end of each as before, leaving the ends slightly open (Fig. 37). Fit these open loops through the end loops on the wire containing the small units, and close by squeezing the loops in flat pliers (Fig. 38).

To make the catch for this necklace, first make a loop at the free end of the right-hand wire in line with the first, then with flat pliers bend outwards at right angles (Fig. 39). Next, at the end of the left-hand wire, make a quarter curve downwards in line with the first (Fig. 40). Then bend this upwards and back into a loop until it nearly touches the main body of the wire (Fig. 41). Thus we have the complete catch (Fig. 42).

The final stage is simply to bend these two wires between the fingers so that they fit the neck and allow the necklace to lie properly.

This is easily done by trying the necklace on, noting where it needs to be bent to make it fit, and carefully adjusting it. Polishing is done by using a brass brush with soap and water as described in the paragraph on finishing.

Pendant

This pendant is designed for the average neck and to fit fairly high. If it is to be made for a larger or smaller neck, or if it is desired to have it hanging lower, you can adjust the side wires. This can easily be done in the final stages.

Fig. 43

Fig. 44

Fig. 45

Fig. 46

The total length of wire required: 6′2″.

Cut 7 lengths of wire 1¾″ long and straighten between the fingers.

Take one of these wires and, using the middle of the jaws of the round nosed pliers, make a loop in each end as in the previous exercise. These loops should be in line and have their joins on the same side (Fig. 43). If they are not in line, hold one of the loops in the flat pliers and with the round pliers twist the other into the correct position.

Bend all the wires in the same way.

The units should all be the same length when complete. If any are too long, cut a small piece out of one of their loops (Fig. 44), and bend further round until the end touches once more (Fig. 45). Repeat if necessary until the length is correct.

Next cut 8 lengths of wire each 1¾″ long and bend loops as before, checking again for equal length of all.

When this second batch of wire units is completed, cut 9 lengths of wire 1⅝″ long and bend as before.

Finally, cut 10 lengths of wire each 1½″ long and this time put a loop in only one end of each (Fig. 46).

The finishing of these last units is easier at this stage than when assembled, so it is advisable to remove now the burrs left on the free ends by the cutting. This is done by rubbing the ends on wet and dry emery paper, placed on a flat surface. Rotate the wires as you rub, leaning them slightly from the vertical so that the sharp edges are bevelled away. Take care not to rub more than just the ends, so that the polished surfaces will not be damaged.

Fig. 47

To make the first of the assembly wires which will hold the units together, cut a length of wire $2\frac{1}{8}''$ long, and straighten. Put a loop at one end using the middle of the jaws of the round pliers (Fig. 47).

On to this wire thread one of the units with only one loop, then one of the longest double looped units (Fig. 48). Carry on in this fashion, threading each of these two types alternatively and finishing with a one looped unit. Throughout assembly keep the joints so that they will finally all hang on one side.

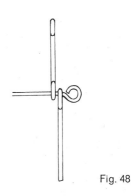

Fig. 48

When properly threaded, make a loop which is in line with the first in the free end of the wire so that the two loops hold the units in place. These should be held together but free enough to be able to swing (Fig. 49).

For the next assembly wire, cut a 2" length of wire and make a loop at one end as before. The next units to be

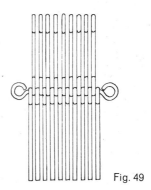

Fig. 49

Fig. 50

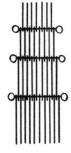

Fig. 51

Fig. 52

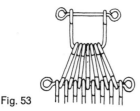

Fig. 53

threaded on are the second longest double looped ones. Starting with one of the units already attached and then one of the new units, this alternating sequence is then carried through, finishing as begun with an attached unit (Fig. 50). When threaded correctly, make a loop in the free end as before.

For the last assembly wire, cut another 2″ length of wire and put a loop in one end. Then thread the remaining units as in the previous stage and make a securing loop at the free end (Fig. 51).

To make the top U shaped link of the pendant, cut a 2″ length of wire and $\frac{3}{4}$″ from one end bend at right angles (Fig. 52). Thread the long side through the top loops and bend at right angles with your fingers where the wire comes out of the loops (Fig. 53). The U of wire formed should have equal sides, but if unequal, cut a little off the longest until correct. Then make a loop at each end so that they are parallel and maintain their equal heights (Fig. 53).

For the first of the neck wires, cut a $1\frac{1}{2}$″ length of wire and put a loop in one end. Thread it through the two loops of the U link and put a securing loop at the free end in line with the first (Fig. 53).

To make the final part of the pendant, which is the long neck wires, cut two lengths of wire each 8″ long. Straighten these between your fingers and make a loop at one end of each piece, using the widest part of the jaws of your round nosed pliers.

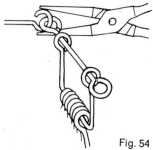

Fig. 54

Fit these loops through the ones on the top wire of the pendant and close with flat pliers (Fig. 54).

To make the catch which will join the remaining two ends of the neck wire at the back of the neck, follow the instructions given in the previous necklace exercise. When this is done, carefully bend each of the neck wires with your fingers until they are the correct shape to fit your neck and allow the pendant to hang properly. The best way to do this is by patiently trying the pendant on several times, noting where it needs to be bent and doing so a little at a time.

Finally when the pendant fits correctly, polish with a brass brush and soapy water as described earlier.

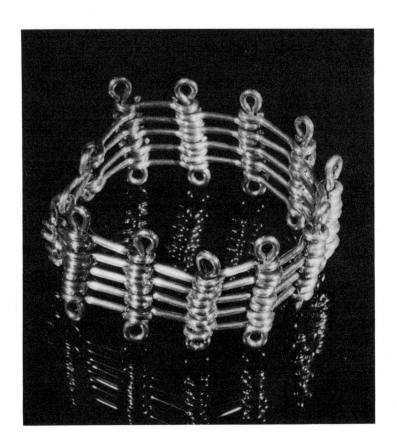

Bracelet

This simple wire bracelet is designed to fit an average adult wrist, but its construction allows it to be easily adapted to fit varying sizes of wrist. Again this bracelet could be worn by a child, and to adjust the length according to the fitting desired is very easily done when assembling the links together.

Length of wire required: 6'9"

Cut 49 lengths of wire each 1¼" long. Care should be taken to make all lengths the same.

Using the middle of the jaws of the round pliers, make a loop at each end of all the wires. These loops should be in line and have their joins on the same side (Fig. 55).

Fig. 55

When all the links are complete, sort them into groups of four and five, making each group from links equal in length. For the assembly wire which will join them together, cut ten lengths of wire 1½" long and put a loop in one end of each.

Fig. 56

Taking one of these wires, thread on nine links so that all joins are at the rear when the alternative links are in opposite directions (Fig. 56).

Fig. 57

When the links are threaded correctly, make a securing loop at the free end of the assembly wire in line with the first (Fig. 57).

Leaving the end with four links free, make the next connection through the five loops. Again keeping the joins at the rear, insert four links between the five already attached and slip another assembly wire through (Fig. 58). Make a securing loop as before.

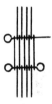

Fig. 58

Next, using five links, begin outside the four previously attached. Thread through the assembly wire and seal with a securing loop (Fig. 59).

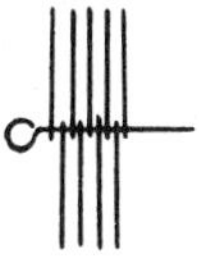

Fig. 59

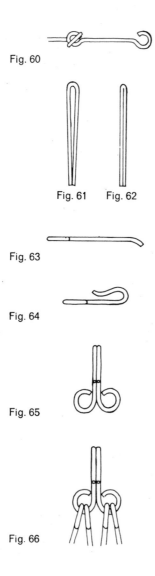

Fig. 60

Fig. 61   Fig. 62

Fig. 63

Fig. 64

Fig. 65

Fig. 66

Continue assembling, using alternative groups of four and five links until you have made the desired length of chain, beginning and ending with four links.

In preparation for the catch, carefully open each of the free end loops until there is enough space to allow the thickness of the wire to pass through (Fig. 60).

To make the hook part of the catch, cut a length of wire 2¾" long. Select the middle and bend in half with the narrow part of the flat pliers, keeping the bend as small as possible (Fig. 61). To close the bend further, hold the wire with round pliers near to the bend and squeeze the loop closed with flat pliers (Fig. 62). With the round pliers, bend the very end of the doubled wire downwards into a quarter circle (Fig. 63). Then bend it upwards and back on itself to form a hook (Fig. 64).

Next separate the two ends of the wire slightly and, with the widest part of the jaws of the round pliers, make two loops (Fig. 65). Slip each of these two loops over two of the opened loops on the links at one end of the bracelet, then close with flat pliers (Fig. 66).

Finally, the loop part of the catch is made by cutting a 2" length of wire and, with the widest part of the jaws of round pliers, making a non-central-

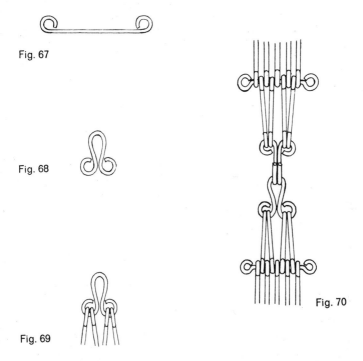

Fig. 67

Fig. 68

Fig. 69

Fig. 70

ized loop at each end so that they are in line (Fig. 67). Then holding the middle in the widest part of the jaws of the round pliers, bend downwards with finger and thumb until loops touch (Fig. 68). When complete, slip each of the two loops over two of the remaining open loops at the free end of the bracelet and close with the flat pliers (Fig. 69). Thus we have the finished catch (Fig. 70).

The bracelet is now complete and ready to be finally finished and polished to your satisfaction.

Necklace

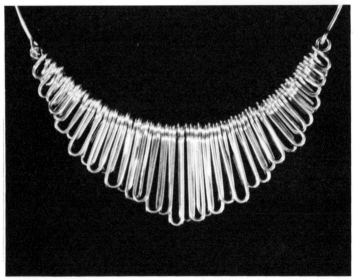

This necklace is designed to fit an average neck size and to hang in a high position. If adjustment is required, this can be carried out as described on p. 17.

The total length of wire
required: 5′ 5¼″

Cut 39 lengths of wire to the
following measurements:

4 lengths at 1½″
4   ,,   ,,   1¾″
4   ,,   ,,   2 ″
4   ,,   ,,   2¼″
4   ,,   ,,   2½″
4   ,,   ,,   2¾″
4   ,,   ,,   3 ″
4   ,,   ,,   3¼″
4   ,,   ,,   3½″
3   ,,   ,,   3¾″

Straighten each piece
between your fingers. Then,
using the centre of the
jaws of the round pliers, make a
loop at each end of all pieces
so that they are in line and
have their joins on the same
side (Fig. 71). If not in line,
twist into correct position with
the flat pliers.

When this is done, take each
unit in turn and by holding
the centre in the widest part of
the jaws of the round pliers
(Fig. 72), bend round into a U
shape with finger and thumb
(Fig. 73). The sides of this U
must be equal and the two
loops parallel to each other
(Fig. 74). If not parallel,
correct by twisting with flat
pliers.

When all units are complete
to this stage, divide the 39
units into two groups, both
having two of each size
excepting for the largest unit,
of which there will only be
one. Lay each of these

Fig. 71

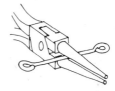

Fig. 72

Fig. 73

Fig. 74

Fig. 75

Fig. 76

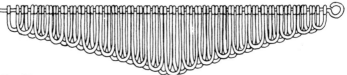

Fig. 77

groups out on a flat surface so that the joins are at the back and the units lie side by side in a graduated line of sizes, progressing from smallest to largest and back to the smallest (Figs. 75 and 76).

The next stage of assembly is to place the first group, which is the longest, under the second. This is done by placing the units from the latter group on top of the first, so that each unit links or overlaps one unit of the same size and one of the next size along (Fig. 77).

32

When the units are properly arranged, cut a 6″ length of wire for the assembly spine which will hold these units together. Make a loop in one end of this wire, using the wide part of the jaws of the round pliers, and thread through all the loops of the carefully arranged units (Fig. 77).

Fig. 78

In the free end of the assembly wire, make a similar loop in line with the first, so that the units are contained between the two loops. Finally, with your fingers, gently bend the wire with the units on it into a curve to suit the neck, keeping the two securing loops so that they will lay flat. (See photograph of necklace).

Fig. 79

For the two neck wires cut two lengths of 6¾″. Straighten and make a loop in one end of each wire, using the widest part of the jaws of the round pliers and leaving them slightly open (Fig. 78).

Fig. 80

Fit these open loops through the end loops of the wire with the units on it, and close by squeezing with the flat pliers (Fig. 79).

Fig. 81

At the free end of the right-hand neck wire, make a quarter circular curve downwards in line with the loop. Then bend the wire upwards and back until the curve almost touches the main body of the wire (Fig. 80).

At the free end of the left-hand neck wire, make a

Fig. 82

loop in line with the first then, using your flat pliers, bend this loop outwards at right angles (Fig. 81). Thus we have the completed catch (Fig. 82).

The final stage is carefully to bend these two neck wires between your fingers until they fit the neck, so allowing the necklace to hang correctly.

Polishing is done as described previously.

More wire jewelry

After making some of the pieces described in this chapter, you should have sufficient experience in working with wire to experiment confidently with ideas of your own. In the photograph on p. 6 you will see examples of other shapes which can easily be made at home and which may help you to begin developing your ideas. Most of these shapes are made either by simply bending with pliers or by first bending the wire round such objects as a pencil (Fig. 83).

There are a great many possibilities to be found in the working of wire shapes, and much enjoyment can be had in making a piece of jewelry which is entirely your own creation from start to finish.

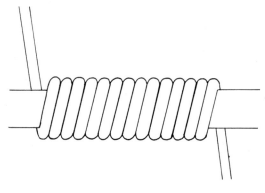

Fig. 83

3 Sheet metal jewelry without soldering

The aim of this chapter is to introduce the reader to working in sheet metal, which is the second of the two main forms in which metal is generally sold. The type of jewelry produced by using just sheet metal differs in so far as it is necessarily constructed of planes, as compared to the lighter linear forms of the wire used in the previous exercises. The following exercises therefore are selected so that the simple methods of working sheet metal, cutting, drilling, bending etc., will become familiar, and this knowledge will be used later in combining both wire and sheet in more complex jewelry.

Materials

Sheet metal is sold in a varying number of sizes and thicknesses, but generally the amount which you will require is small and so it is impractical to go out and buy a whole sheet of metal.

When buying silver sheet you need only ask for the actual size that you require, which can be worked out from the details given in each exercise. Any scrap silver that is left when you have finished making the piece of jewelry should be carefully saved. When sufficient is collected, you can return it to the dealer who will buy it back at slightly less than you paid for it. This will help to keep costs down.

This procedure, however, does not apply to buying copper or any other non-precious metal, and copper is usually sold in complete sheet form, which is expensive. It is therefore a good idea to find a local supplier who sells small pieces or off-cuts, because buying in this way will prove much more convenient.

The required thickness or gauge of the sheet for the following pieces will be approximately 1/16th inch. Do not buy metal thicker than this, as it will be difficult to work with and make your jewelry too heavy. Also, when selecting a piece of metal, try to avoid any which is deeply scratched, as this will cause you extra work when polishing.

Tools

The following supplementary tools must be added to your

collection in order that metal can be successfully worked.

Bench peg or pin

This is a piece of reasonably hard wood which is fixed to the working surface so that it projects at right angles by about four inches and forms a convenient working edge on which to saw and file.

The actual proportions of the peg or pin may vary slightly according to the reader's convenience, but as a guide select a piece of rectangular wood 9″ x 3″ and approximately $\frac{1}{2}$″ thick. In the centre of one of the 3″ sides cut a V which is $1\frac{1}{2}$″ deep and $1\frac{1}{2}$″ wide (Fig. 84). If you have no wood working tools, ask the man from whom you buy it to cut it to shape for you.

To hold this bench pin firmly in its place on your working surface and so as not to damage the table with screws, it will be necessary to buy a small G cramp (C clamp in the U.S.A., where bench pin and clamp can be bought in a combined unit). This can be used to clamp the bench pin to the hardboard and table top (Fig. 85) and can then be removed with the hardboard surface when not required.

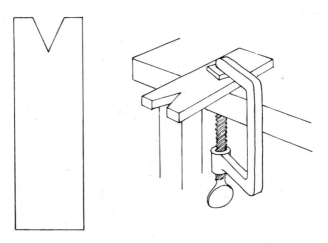

Fig. 84   Fig. 85

Sawing

One of the most useful jeweller's tools is the piercing saw, which can be bought at retailers specialising in jeweller's tools. This type of saw is unique, for unlike other metal saws it has a very fine blade held in a comparatively deep frame, which allows the direction of the cutting to change as many times as desired.

The saw looks similar to a small fretwork saw and is composed of two parts, a light steel frame and a thin blade which is easily detachable and replaceable. Many grades of blades are available, but if the gauge of metal suggested is used, then grade 1/0 is correct. If, however, the metal used is thinner or thicker, then the general rule of three teeth of the blade to the thickness of the metal will give you the correct grade to use.

To prepare the saw for use, first place one end of the blade in the top clamp of the saw frame so that the teeth are facing frontwards, away from the inside of the frame and downwards, then tighten the clamp. Next hold the saw so that the top arm of the frame rests firmly in the V of the bench pin and press the frame so that the two ends come slightly together. Place the other end of the blade in the bottom clamp and tighten (Fig. 86). Release pressure on the frame and the blade should now be held in tension.

The saw is now ready to use. Hold the metal flat on the bench pin so that the line to be cut is over the V.

Position yourself with the right hand holding the saw upright behind the line to be cut. Begin to saw by moving

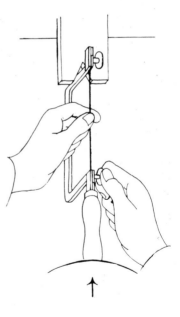

Fig. 86

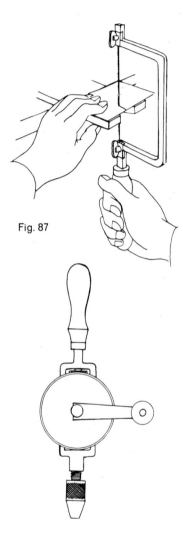

Fig. 87

Fig. 88

the saw up and down using the full length of the blade and keeping the saw vertical. Do not let the saw lean from the vertical or try to rush the cutting, because overstraining the blade will result in it breaking (Fig. 87).

When cutting a curve, turn the metal progressively round, keeping the saw in a fairly constant cutting position.

Where it is desired to cut out an inside shape, drill a small hole inside the line, thread the blade through and cut out as before.

Drilling

A small hand drill is required and these are easily obtainable in a range of sizes from most tool dealers. There is no reason to buy the expensive larger type, as the amount and kind of drilling required is not sufficient to warrant it. Choose one of the smaller types of hand drills which are reasonably priced (Fig. 88).

The actual drills, or bits as they are sometimes called, can also be purchased from tool shops, and are sold either in sets or separately. For our purpose, a small set of four drills will be sufficient, and they should be the following sizes: 1/32″ diameter, 1/16″, 3/32″ and 1/8″.

The final tool that you will need in preparation for drilling is the centre punch. This punch is simply a short length of hardened steel rod which has a point ground at one end. To use, place the point at the position required for drilling on the metal then, holding the punch upright, gently tap with a hammer, so making a small indentation in the surface of the metal. This indentation acts as a starting guide to the drill and stops it from wandering from the correct place (Fig. 89).

Fig. 89

Filing

In order that sawn edges can be smoothed and finally shaped, at this stage you will need to buy a few files. Files are sold in a great variety of shapes, sizes and grades of cut, but for the purpose of the following exercises two sorts are required, hand files and needle files. The hand files needed are of the 8″ smooth cut type, one flat and the other a Suage file (Fig. 90).

Needle files are smaller than the hand type, and are useful where the larger ones cannot conveniently be used. The needle files required are half round and square (Fig. 91).

Another tool you will need here is the scriber. This is simply a small steel tool with a sharp point ground at one end and is used to mark lines on to metal (Fig. 92).

Fig. 90

Fig. 91

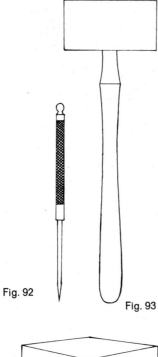

Fig. 92

Fig. 93

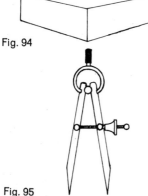

Fig. 94

Fig. 95

A small boxwood mallet is a useful tool for straightening any bent metal, and this type of mallet should have two flat ends (Fig. 93).

You will also need a flat steel surface block to mallet on. This should have a polished smooth surface without deep scratches, because if it is marked the surface of the metal being malleted will be damaged. There are suitable, small, polished steel jewellers' blocks sold in shops specializing in jewellers' tools, and these measure approximately 3″ square by 1″ thick (Fig. 94). It is not absolutely necessary to buy one of these blocks, for any polished flat steel surface of a reasonable size can be used. One of the older type of flat irons, with the handle cut off so that it can stand on your bench, would prove completely satisfactory. Another way to save on expenditure is to use an off-cut of steel plate of more than $\frac{1}{4}$″ thick, which has had all the sharp edges removed. A local metal dealer may be able to help you here.

The final tool you will need is a pair of dividers (Fig. 95). These are similar to a pencil compass except that both ends are pointed, and they are used to mark metal.

Hairslide

The hairslide is the first item which uses copper or silver in the form of sheet metal instead of wire. Although very simple to make, it does mark a step forward in learning the craft of jewelry making because it involves the use of the piercing saw. This is an important cutting tool because of its versatility, and once you have learnt to use it properly it will enable you to tackle a much wider range of articles.

The actual shape of the hairslide and type of decoration used can easily be varied to suit your own ideas without entailing any drastic deviation from the instructions given. The size of the pieces of sheet metal that you will need for this hairslide are as follows:- one rectangle, 2¾" x 1¾", and another ⅜" x 3½". If not flat, put a piece of paper on either side of the sheet metal and, placing it on the steel block, gently mallet it until flat. Take care not to mark the surface unnecessarily.

Taking the larger piece, first mark out the shape to be cut out. This is done by placing a piece of tracing paper over the full size drawing (Fig. 96) and carefully making a tracing. Then in order that the outline can be transferred to the metal, shade with a soft pencil where the lines show through on the reverse side of the tracing paper. Next, using a small piece of plasticine, roll it over the metal surface so that it leaves a slight deposit of plasticine which will allow the marks of the tracing to show. Place your tracing carefully in position on the metal surface, hold it still and draw over the lines with a fairly hard pencil. Take your tracing off and you will find an impression of the shape on the metal. This impression is very easily smudged and would soon be ruined if used as a guide when sawing, so it is necessary to go over the lines carefully with a scriber. In this way the lines will be lightly scratched into the surface of the metal and will serve as a more permanent indication. However, do not scribe deeply or unnecessarily because the marks may have to be removed when polishing.

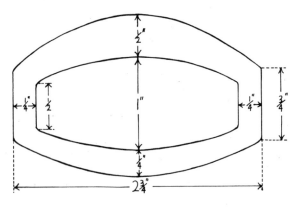

Fig. 96

42

Once the first part of your clip is satisfactorily marked out, you are ready to cut it out with the piercing saw. It is advisable to have a few practice cuts before beginning on the actual clip, so try cutting a few straight and curved lines on an odd piece of metal. When confident, begin to cut out the outer shape of the clip. Cut slightly on the outside of the line, turning the metal as the curves are cut. When a corner is reached, do not force the blade to turn, but continue moving the saw up and down in one spot, slowly turning the metal and giving the blade time to cut a small space for itself as it turns. Then, as the required angle is reached, proceed as before until cutting is complete (Fig. 97).

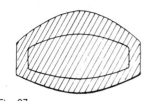

Fig. 97

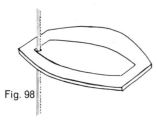

Fig. 98

If there is a tendency for the saw to jam when cutting, it will help to lubricate the blade by rubbing it now and then with a piece of beeswax or candle grease.

To cut out the inside shape, first select a position just inside the line to be cut and centre punch it lightly. Using a 1/16" diameter drill, drill a hole at this spot.

Undo the top clamp of the saw, so releasing the blade which is then threaded through the hole in the metal (Fig. 98). Place the blade back in the top of the clamp, press the saw frame against the bench pin and tighten the clamp to retension the blade.

Cut the inside shape out as before, leaving this part of the clip ready to be filed to its final shape (Fig. 99).

To file the outer edge, use the flat 8" file. Hold the clip endways against the bench pin and file lengthways along the edges, moving the file in sympathy with the shape. In

Fig. 99

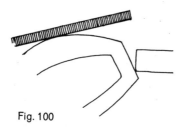

Fig. 100

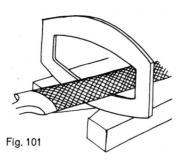

Fig. 101

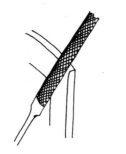

Fig. 102

this way you will avoid any unwanted facets (Fig. 100).

To file the two curved edges of the inside shape, use the shallow curved face of the 8″ Suage file. When filing an inside shape such as this, which requires the file to be used at approximately right angles across the edge, it is advisable to keep the file moving sideways along the edge, as well as across (Fig. 101). This action results in a smoother contour, but take care not to cut into the two end flats of the inside shape. These flats can be filed separately with the flat of the half round needle file.

When the initial filing is done and you are satisfied that the shape is true, remove any burrs and sharp edges. This is done by using the half round needle file to file carefully along each edge, slightly rounding it (Fig. 102).

When the first part of the hair clip is complete to this stage, put it aside and begin the remaining part, which is the long central pin to go through the hair.

When marking out this pin, there is no need to make a tracing this time. As only straight lines are needed, simply mark the measurements given straight on to the surface of the metal, using a scriber (Fig. 103).

Begin piercing out the pin,

again cutting slightly outside
the line so that there is a
little left to file off finally. In
cutting a long shape like this,
which is longer than the depth
of the saw frame, you will find
it necessary to cut from each
end towards a central meeting
point.

After cutting is completed,
use the flat face of the half
round file to file the edges
lengthways as before. File over
the central point left on each
long side, so that the whole
edge takes on a slow curve
(Fig. 104).

The two ends should be filed
square to the sides and then
the corners lightly rounded.

Finally remove all burrs and
sharp edges.

To mark out the decorative
motif on the larger part of the
hair clip, first find half the
length of the thicker side, then
the middle of the width at
that point. Mark this position
by gently centre punching it,
then, with your dividers,
scribe a circle with a radius
of $\frac{1}{8}''$. Divide the circumference
of this circle into eight equal
parts, as shown in Fig. 105.
Centre punch each one of
these divisions and scribe
a line connecting each one
to the central mark (Fig. 105).
Using a 1/32" diameter drill,
carefully drill a hole at each of
these points. When this is done,
cut the straight lines connecting
each of these outer holes to the

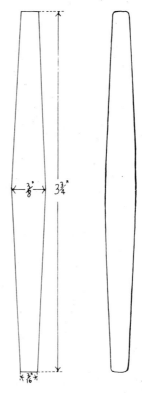

Fig. 103   Fig. 104

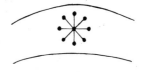

Fig. 105

45

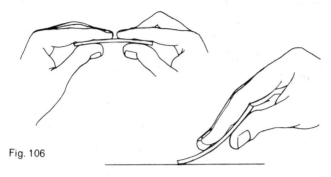

Fig. 106

Fig. 107

centre one. This is done by threading the piercing blade through each outer hole in turn and sawing along the lines to the central hole.

The hand polishing of sheet metal jewelry differs slightly from the procedure used for wire jewelry. Any marks on the larger surfaces show much more, so these must be removed completely if a polish is to be obtained. The correct way is first to place the jewelry on a sheet of paper and with wet and dry emery paper and water as a lubricant, rub the surfaces until all scratches are removed. If the scratches are deep, use a slightly coarser wet and dry paper first, then the smoother.

When all marks are removed, place the jewelry on a clean sheet of paper and rub the surfaces with the fluffy side of a small piece of leather, applying metal polish liberally. When a satisfactory polish is obtained, clean with a soft duster.

To form the parts of the hair clip into the final shape, gently bend each part between your fingers or, by bending against your working surface, slowly work from the ends inwards towards the middle, keeping the curve uniform (Figs. 106 and 107). Remember that where the motif has been cut, the metal will be weakened and inclined to bend too much if not handled carefully.

Bracelet

This bracelet is designed to fit an average sized wrist fairly
loosely, but it is advisable to check the measurements of
your own wrist before beginning. This is easily done by
asking a friend to pass a piece of string around your wrist
so that it is just slightly loose. Use this measurement, adding
one inch more to give the correct loose fit required for com-
fort and manipulation of the catch. Check this total length
against the measurements given on the following page, and
if different, adjust the length according to your own requirements.

The length of metal you will need for this bracelet is a strip $\frac{1}{2}''$ wide and $7\frac{1}{2}''$ long. If you cannot buy such a strip exactly to size, any suitably flat piece into which the blank can be fitted should be used. It will be a help, however, if a piece with one straight side can be found, as this will save you having to cut one side.

Mark out the bracelet by scribing a rectangle of the size required (Fig. 108).

To cut out this·strip, which is longer than the saw frame is deep, a slight modification to the saw blade is necessary so that it is possible to cut the whole length of the strip. Fit the blade normally, i.e., so that it is in tension and the teeth face forwards and downwards. Then, using your flat nosed pliers, at each end of the blade, about $\frac{1}{4}''$ from the clamps of the saw frame, gently twist the blade until the teeth face at right angles to the frame (Figs 109 and 110).

Having made this adjustment to the blade of the saw, you will find that the cutting action will be the same, except that the frame is now held at right angles to the saw cut, as opposed to directly behind as before (Fig. 111).

Using the saw in this way, cut out the strip, keeping the saw cut slightly on the outside of the line and straight.

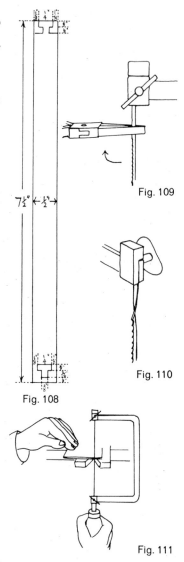

Fig. 109

$7\frac{1}{2}''$ ← $\frac{1}{2}''$ →

Fig. 110

Fig. 108

Fig. 111

48

When cut out, using the flat 8″ hand file, file along each edge lengthways, holding the strip against the bench pin. Try to keep the long sides as straight and as parallel as possible, and the two ends at right angles to them. To finish the two long edges properly, lay a sheet of wet and dry emery paper on a flat surface, and using water as a lubricant, rub them across the paper, keeping the strip upright. Continue rubbing down each side until all file marks have disappeared.

Finally, remove any burrs and slightly round all edges with the flat side of a half round needle file.

At one end of your metal strip, mark out the first part of the catch, using a scriber (Fig. 112).

Change the saw blade back as for normal use, and carefully cut out the tongue part of the catch. Finish the shape with a square needle file and slightly round the corners as shown (Fig. 113).

When complete, use flat pliers to bend the tab upwards until at right angles (Fig. 114).

At the other end of your strip, mark out the negative part of the catch (Fig 115). If any mistakes have been made in the thicknesses of the first part of the catch, adjust sizes accordingly so that a good fit is certain.

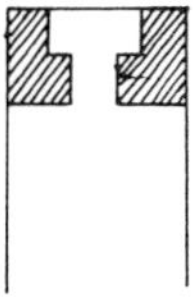

Fig. 112

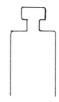

Fig. 113

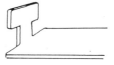

Fig. 114

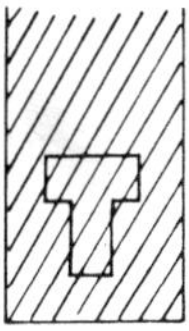

Fig. 115

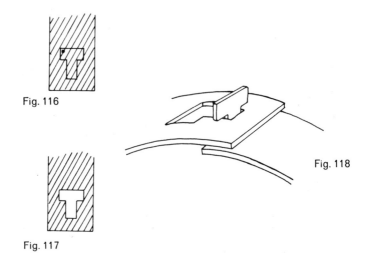

Fig. 116

Fig. 118

Fig. 117

Centre punch a point just inside the top line of the upper shape and drill a hole using a 1/16″ diameter drill (Fig. 116). Thread the blade of the saw through the hole and cut out, sawing slightly inside the line and finishing the shape with a square needle file (Fig. 117). Check with the dividers that the first part of the clip will fit, and if too small, file until correct fit is obtained. (See complete catch, Fig. 118.)

The polishing of the bracelet should now be done before it is finally bent into shape. To polish, use the same method as in previous exercise. First remove all scratches with wet and dry paper, then polish with leather and metal polish.

When you are satisfied that the finish is good enough, begin to bend the bracelet with your fingers into an oval to suit your wrist. Do not use pliers as these will mark. Do not hurry the bending, but work systematically, beginning at each end and working inwards. Remember that the catch should go at the centre on the inside of the wrist, and that where the negative part of the catch has been cut, the metal is much thinner and will bend easily unless handled carefully.

4 Soldering, findings and stones

You are now ready to make jewelry that combines both the qualities and methods of the two previous chapters together with other simple techniques, such as lead soldering. For this reason, you can make a much larger range of articles. However, as it is obviously impossible to include every type of jewelry, the selection given is aimed at extending the variety of the articles in this book, rather than duplicating earlier pieces.

Lead soldering

One of the easiest ways of strongly joining two pieces of metal together is to lead solder them. This is a solder which melts at a very low temperature, so making it more practical to use in the home than other methods of soldering, which require much higher temperatures.

To lead solder you will first need a place to solder on which will take the heat used without burning. A small sheet of asbestos approximately 6" x 4" x ¼" thick is ideal, and can be obtained at retailers dealing in jeweller's tools or at some local tool shops.

Soldering can be safely done on many table tops without harm, though polished surfaces should be avoided as even slight heat may damage them. To insulate the table from the heat, find a piece

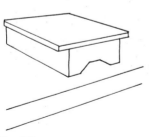

of old fire brick or any similar item which can withstand heat and is two or more inches thick. Put this on your hardboard working surface in a convenient position near the edge, then place on top your piece of asbestos sheet (Fig. 119). Do not use the hard building type of asbestos which may crack when heated, but the soft fibrous type used for iron rests etc.

Fig. 119

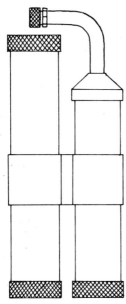

Fig. 120

To solder satisfactorily it is necessary to heat the parts to be joined together to the same temperature. If one part is hotter than the other, the solder will run on to that part only, so making a mess and ruining the surface. As jewelry is generally made of pieces of metal of various sizes, and the larger pieces will require more heat than the smaller parts, to solder successfully a method of heating must be used which is adaptable enough to heat these varying pieces evenly. The best tool to use for making jewelry at home is a small flame torch of the kind which uses methylated spirits and has a small, fine, hot flame. (It is called a Burngomatic in the U.S.A.) These can be obtained at tool shops and are inexpensive (Fig. 120). Be careful to follow the instruction given with each torch and to store it in a safe place away from fires when not in use.

Electric soldering irons, which are normally used for soldering electrical equipment, are not generally satisfactory in jewelry making because not enough heat can be properly transferred to the pieces being soldered.

The most convenient way to buy lead solder is in a wire form such as is sold in many shops. It will probably have a small core of flux running

Fig. 121

through its centre (Fig. 121), but you will also require a small tin of flux to supplement this. Either a liquid or a paste type of lead flux will be suitable, but remember not to get any on your hands as it will irritate a sensitive skin and should be washed off immediately if you do. Flux is used to keep the surface of the metal clean, so allowing the solder to run properly.

The final extra tool that you will need when soldering is a pair of tweezers. These can be used to manipulate the hot pieces of metal whilst soldering and to place the small pieces of solder in place. Almost any tweezers will do as long as they are not aluminium, which will melt. Good steel or brass pairs can be bought from most tool shops (Fig. 122).

It will help you to have one or two practice solderings before beginning properly, and the secret of good soldering is as follows: - (a) The joint to be soldered must be a good fit and not have gaps showing (Fig. 123). (b) All surfaces must be clean. (c) All surfaces to be joined must have flux on them. (d) Enough, but not too much, solder should be placed on the joint. (e) Both sides of the joint should be heated equally so that the solder runs correctly.

To practice soldering, choose two small pieces of flat sheet

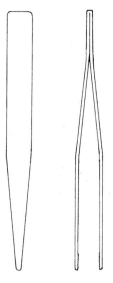

Fig. 122

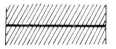

Fig. 123

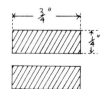

Fig. 124

53

metal which have straight edges (Fig. 124). If you have no odd pieces, then cut two rectangles of sheet approximately $\frac{3}{4}''$ x $\frac{1}{4}''$ and file one edge of each piece straight. Lightly rub the edge and surrounding metal with fine emery paper to clean the surfaces. Then, using a spent match stick, apply a small amount of flux along the two edges. To help heating, before placing the two pieces in position on the asbestos sheet to solder, cut the heads off four 1″ nails and place these so that they will hold the pieces of metal slightly above the asbestos (Fig. 125). To avoid these nails being soldered to your metal, keep them away from the area of the join.

When in position, place the two pieces of sheet on top so that the edges to be joined touch (Fig. 126). Light your torch and begin to heat gently by moving the flame along the joint and keeping both pieces of metal equally heated. When the flux bubbles up and then settles, take the flame away and with your cutters cut a few pieces of lead solder, each about 1/16″ long.

Pick up one of the pieces with tweezers, dip it into the flux and place in the centre of the joint (Fig. 127). Continue heating equally as before, until the solder is seen to flow

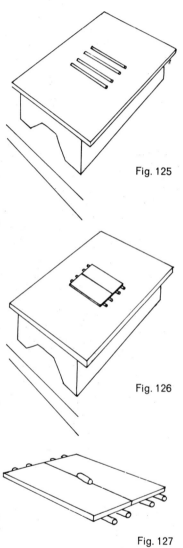

Fig. 125

Fig. 126

Fig. 127

along the joint. If there does not seem to be enough solder to fill the join, apply another piece of solder and reheat. When the joint is satisfactory, leave it to cool for a few minutes so that the solder has time to harden before the practice plate is moved. Finally wash off the flux and remove any excess solder with a fine file. The two pieces of sheet should now be strongly soldered together and the seam should show only as a thin line of lead. Continue practicing until you have gained confidence and feel ready to tackle the soldering in the remaining exercises.

Jeweller's findings

This is a name given to the dozens of various types of small items such as catches, ear clips, etc. that can be bought ready made for use in making jewelry. Their use saves a great deal of time and effort, and though there are times when special pieces have to be made to suit a particular piece, generally a ready made fitting can be found to do the job. These findings are produced in large quantities and are relatively inexpensive.

It will be of benefit to you to familiarise yourself with the different types of fitting available at your nearest stockist, because in making jewelry at home you will find them invaluable. Local jewellers sometimes sell a few, but usually you will need to go to a retailer specialising in jeweller's materials or to a precious metal manufacturer who produces these findings. Often these larger firms will send you illustrations of the types they make and will supply you by mail, though of course you need to make a reasonable order because they often have minimum charges.

In the following chapter only a few of the more common findings are used, but the next page shows a more complete range of some of the other fittings available. These illustrations will help you find a fitting to suit your requirements when repairing or making future jewelry, and for a list of some of the suppliers, see page 95.

One final item which is also sold ready made by these suppliers is chain, available in various kinds of metals. There are a great many types of chain, but twisted and straight linked chain are the two shapes generally seen, and both these can be bought in different sizes varying from fine to heavy.

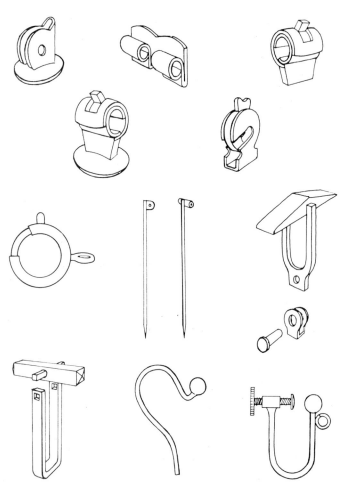

Jeweller's findings, reading down, left to right

Fichu hinge, flat hinge, revolver catch, revolver catch with base, side opening catch, bolt ring, pin to fit fichu hinge, pin to fit flat hinge, swivel cufflinks back, cufflinks back with detachable arm, earwires, earscrews.

Other suitable materials to mount

The use of different materials other than semi-precious and precious stones in jewelry can give very interesting and pleasing results. Only two examples are given in the following pieces, but there is no reason why a piece of ivory, plastic or wood could not be substituted for a stone if you so desire. In fact, your jewelry will gain in personal value if you use something that you really feel is interesting rather than just a ready-cut stone. Many exciting items can be found on beaches or bought for very little in junk shops. A good source of ivory is old billard balls, and broken ornaments can afford a good supply of interesting materials. Some items you will find unsuitable because of their irregular shape, but any item that has a flat side can generally be glued to a suitable piece of jewelry quite successfully. Of course, any soft material such as ivory can be filed to shape, or have a flat side filed on it so that a good fit is ensured. Do remember, however, that when mounting these materials all soldering must be done before glueing, otherwise they may be damaged by the heat.

Glueing

There are many glues on the market, but the most suitable for sticking the various materials used in jewelry is the epoxy resin type of adhesive. This glue can be bought at most ironmongers (hardware stores), and though needing twenty-four hours to harden in normal use, it does give a very strong joint. However, if you are to get satisfactory results, the surfaces to be joined must be clean and slightly rough to help binding. To prepare the glue, a little of the contents of the tube of resin and the tube of hardener should be spread on a clean surface in equal parts and, using a matchstick, mixed until a milky coloured mixture is obtained. Apply a thin coat to each surface of the joint, press together and leave to harden. If any of the glue has spread on to places where it should not be, use a soft piece of rag moistened with water to wipe clean before allowing to dry. It will be difficult to remove the glue once it has dried without spoiling the surfaces of the metal.

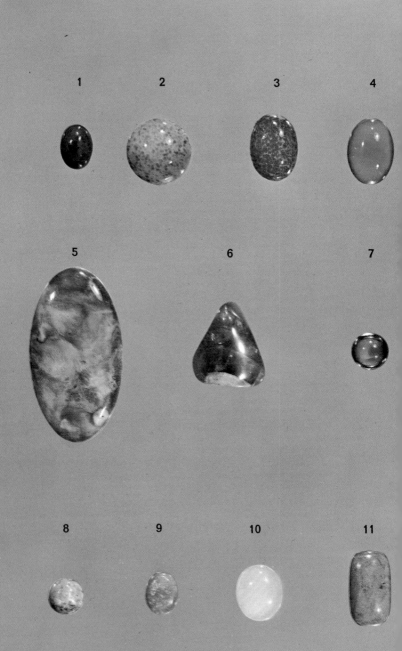

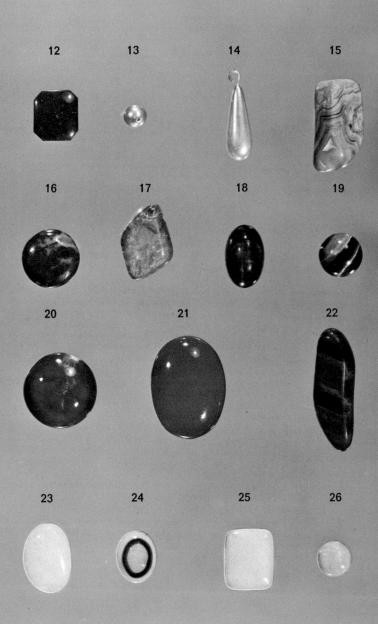

12   13   14   15

16   17   18   19

20   21   22

23   24   25   26

Previous page:

1 Lapis Lazuli; 2 Emerald Matrix; 3 Lapis Lazuli Matrix; 4 Chryso-
prase; 5 Pottery; 6 Amethyst; 7 Amethyst; 8 Turquoise; 9 Opal;
10 Amazonite; 11 Agate; 12 Goldstone; 13 Imitation Pearl; 14 Imita-
tation Drop Pearl; 15 Agate - mineral sample; 16 Agate; 17 Quatzs
- mineral sample; 18 Catseye; 19 Tigers Eye; 20 Pottery; 21 Cor-
nelian; 22 Jasper; 23 Milky Quartz - mineral sample; 24 Onyx;
25 Opal; 26 Opal.

Beads

Many shops stock a variety of plastic and wooden beads,
and these can easily be combined into your jewelry to good
effect.

Though only one example is given in this book, such a
wealth of shapes and colours is obtainable with beads that
they should provide you with plenty of opportunity to make
your own interesting combinations. In general, simple wire
jewelry is the most suited to use with beads, and the earlier
exercises in Chapter 2 may help to give you ideas.

Stones

The types of stones most suited to the jewelry in this book
fall into three categories. They are as follows: semi-precious
stones that have been cut and polished, cut imitation stones,
and uncut but polished stones such as mineral samples.
Except for a few of the semi-precious stones, all are inexpensive and can be bought from a variety of sources. The
best way to begin to collect stones for jewelry making is to
look out for the occasional shop which has them, and to
buy a few that you like each time. In this way you will amass
a good assortment from which to choose, and not really
notice the cost. At this stage there is no real reason to buy a
stone that is expensive, for there are many interesting
stones which will cost very little. If you do have any difficulty
in obtaining stones, a list of suppliers is given on p. 95.

Stones, as you will discover, are cut into many different
shapes, the transparent ones being cut with facets so as to
reflect their colour to their best advantage, and the trans-
lucent and opaque ones more smoothly to show their individual quality (Fig. 128). Each of these shapes needs to

be mounted into jewelry in a certain way so as to show each stone to its best effect, but obviously it is impossible to discuss all these different techniques in this book. The most suitable type of stone to use in jewelry making at home, and which is used in the following pieces, is the opaque type of stone with a flat back, called cabochon cut (below). This type of stone is the easiest to make a setting for, because it lies flat on the metal sheet and, being opaque, does not need to have a complicated setting to allow light to the back of the stone. In fact this type of stone, if so desired, can be glued directly on to a suitable piece of jewelry without any setting to hold it.

Besides those stones which are cut to shape, other suitable and interesting stones, which are mineral samples, can be bought. These polished pieces of stone are usually too irregular in shape to be used generally in jewelry making, and because of this they are usually cheaper than the properly cut stones. These mineral samples can be bought from various sources, but in case of difficulty consult the list of suppliers given on p. 95. Remember, however, when buying them, to restrict yourself to those that have shapes suitable for glueing or setting on to jewelry.

Another way of collecting stones is to look for them on beaches and in the countryside. Often you can pick up interesting ones which are suitable.

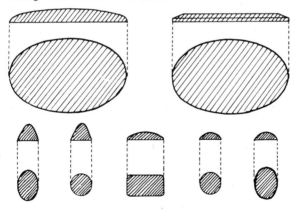

Fig. 128: Suitable cabochon styles of cut stones

Birth stones

Month	Colour	Stone
January	dark red	garnet
February	purple	amethyst
March	pale blue	aquamarine
April	white, transparent	rock crystal
May	bright green	chrysoprase
June	cream	moonstone
July	red	cornelian (carnelian)
August	pale green	sardonyx
September	deep blue	lapis lazuli
October	variagated	opal
November	yellow	topaz
December	sky blue	turquoise

How to keep stones

Once you have begun to collect various stones for your jewelry making, it is best to keep them separate from each other so that they do not knock together and become damaged. Each different type of stone varies in hardness, and if a hard material is allowed to rub against a softer one, the surface of the softer one will become marked or, worse still, they may break if knocked together.

There are many ways of keeping them safe, from wrapping them in tissue paper to buying a special cabinet to put them in, but for little cost and time a suitable store can be made from any strongly made chocolate box. All you need is a few lengths of $\frac{1}{8}''$ thick balsa wood and a tube of glue. The balsa wood can be cut to fit into the box, and glued into place so that the box is divided into small shallow compartments to take each stone. In this way stones can be safely kept (Fig. 129).

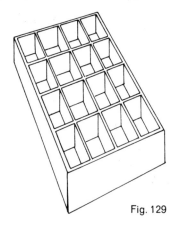

Fig. 129

Choosing the stones to use

One of the first things you will discover when buying stones to use for the following pieces is that in most cases it is impossible to find stones that are exactly the same as those used in this book. This is because, except for manufactured stones, the stones originally came from pieces of material which were different in size, and as the cutting and polishing was done in a way to save the maximum of material for the finished stone, most stones are necessarily individual. In fact it is very difficult to find even two stones that are exactly the same, so buy stones which you like and which are as similar as you can conveniently find. Basically, any stone can be substituted for the ones used in these pieces, as long as it has a flat back and some resemblance to the size and shape. Obviously, therefore, it is impossible to give exact instructions for all the varying stones and when following the exercises, use the instructions given purely as an example of how to make the setting for your own stone. To adapt the instructions to your own needs, simply substitute measurements relating to your own stone.

5 Jewelry combining various methods

Brooch

This brooch uses a large, blue, oval pottery stone, 1¾″ long and 1″ wide. This is a manufactured stone made by shaping in a mould and glazed with pottery glaze, and it is likely that you will be able to buy one that is exactly the same size from a craft shop or similar supplier. However, if you find difficulty in obtaining one, buy instead any suitable shallow cabochon cut stone that is approximately the same size, and adjust the measurements given to those of your own stone. There are, for instance, some very interesting agate stones of a similar proportion which can be bought fairly easily, and though more expensive, they will make a very satisfactory substitute.

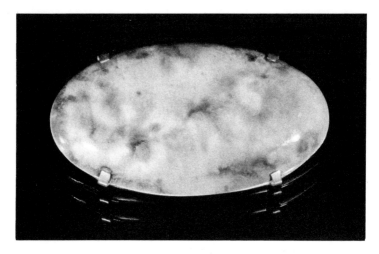

The piece of metal that you will require for this brooch is a flat rectangle of metal, gauge 18 or thinner and slightly larger than your stone. In the case of this pottery stone, it needs to be 2″ x 1⅛″.

Place your stone in the centre of the sheet of metal and use a scriber to mark a line round it. Remove the stone and mark half the length of each short side of the metal sheet, then scribe a line to each of these points, so dividing the shape of the stone equally (Fig. 130).

To mark out the position of the claws which will hold the stone on to this back plate, start at one corner and pencil a line inwards so that it joins the shape of the stone at right angles (Fig. 131).

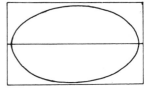

Fig. 130

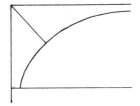

Fig. 131

When you are satisfied that it is correct, mark it with your scriber. Then, with your pair of dividers, measure the distance from the centre line to the line you have just made (Fig. 132). Using this same measurement, mark the three remaining positions for the claws and scribe a line as before (Fig. 133). Mark out each of these claws so that they are $\frac{1}{8}''$ wide and the length you will need to hold the stone in place.

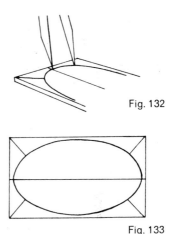

Fig. 132

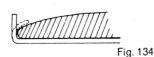

Fig. 133

To judge the length, place the stone on a flat surface and measure a suitable length for the claw to bend over the edge of the stone as shown in Fig. 134. For the stone used here, the correct length is 3/16" (Fig. 135).

When you have done this, saw out the shape with your piercing saw, cutting just outside the lines (Fig. 136).

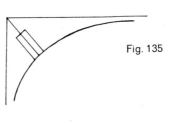

Fig. 134

Try your stone on the cut shape and file it to fit exactly, remembering that the stone should be tried the same way round each time because it may not be true. When the metal fits the shape of the stone, smooth all edges, first using a needle file then polishing with very fine emery paper wrapped round a suitable file. Finally, polish the back, removing any scratches.

When polished satisfactorily, use flat pliers to bend each of the claws up at right angles.

Fig. 135

Fig. 136

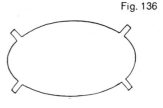

Fig. 137

Fig. 138

Fig. 139

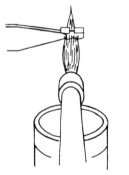

Fig. 140

Be careful to bend as close to where the stone will sit as possible (Fig. 137).

So that the claws will not appear too clumsy, and to make the setting of the stone easier, they should now be filed into taper (Fig. 138). This should be done with the flat side of a needle file, taking care not to scratch any surrounding surfaces.

The next step in making the brooch is the clip. For this you will need three jeweller's findings, a 1½″ long pin, a suitable hinge (joint) and a swivel type of safety catch (Fig. 139). Actually, various types of these fittings can be used with the same result, so if you can only buy other sorts of pins etc., the following method of assembly will apply equally as well.

The first part of the clip to solder on is the hinge (joint). This is done by fluxing the side to be soldered, then placing two small pieces of lead solder also fluxed into position. Hold the hinge with tweezers and put it in the flame of your torch (Fig. 140). Wait for the solder just to become molten, then remove and allow it to cool. Do not overheat the solder, or it will flow into the hinge and spoil it.

Put the brooch with the back upmost on to your asbestos sheet. Flux where the hinge is to be soldered and put the hinge in position approximately $\frac{1}{4}''$ from the edge.

Gently heat until the flux bubbles and then settles. If the hinge has moved, push it back into place with your tweezers.

Begin to heat again by playing the flame on to the sheet metal back, because this will need more heating than the hinge itself (Fig. 141). Probably sufficient heat will transfer to the hinge to make the solder flow neatly under it, but if not, when the back is hot pass the flame over the hinge a few times to bring it up to the same heat. Do not overheat either piece, and as soon as the solder does form a good join take the flame away and allow to cool, before washing off flux.

The next part of the clip to solder on is the catch. It is important not to use too much solder in doing this, and not to overheat when soldering, because otherwise the working parts of the catch may become soldered solid and useless.

As before with the hinge, flux the base and, placing a small amount of solder in position, heat it in your flame until the solder just runs.

So that the catch will sit upright in its correct place on the back plate, it may be necessary to file a small flat on the blob of solder (Fig. 142). Reflux the catch and also

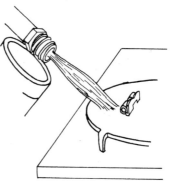

Fig. 141

Fig. 142

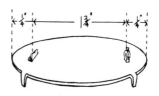

Fig. 143

63

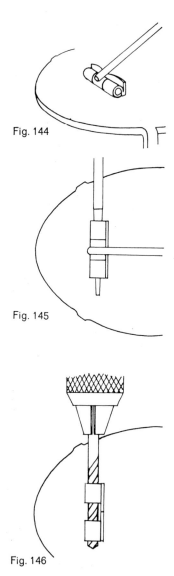

Fig. 144

Fig. 145

Fig. 146

flux the back plate where it is to be soldered on $\frac{1}{4}''$ from the edge (Fig. 143). Heat, allowing the flux to settle, reposition if necessary and solder as before, keeping your flame mainly on the back of the brooch. Be careful not to heat the hinge which is already soldered. If the solder does unfortunately run on to the catch because of unequal heating, so making it useless, lift it off with tweezers whilst the solder is still molten and begin again with a new catch.

The next part of the catch to fit is the pin, which should be slightly longer than the space between the two fittings you have just soldered on. First, at the hinge end of the pin, there is a small tube which has to be filed to fit into the hinge part already soldered on. This is done by filing either side of the tube until it fits snugly between the two tubes of the hinge part (Fig. 144).

To hold the pin in the hinge (joint), it is next necessary to make a small hinge pin (ribet). This is made from a piece of 3/16″ wire filed to a slow taper at one end so that it pushes into the holes in the hinge (Fig. 145). If when soldering these holes became blocked, carefully drill them clear, using a 1/32″ drill. You will find that the lead solder blocking the holes can be removed easily when drilling

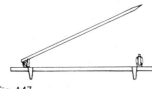

Fig. 147

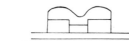

Fig. 148

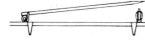

Fig. 149

Fig. 150

and needs very little pressure (Fig. 146). (In the U.S.A. pins can be bought with the ribet wire attached.)

When you have the taper pin (ribet wire) fitting correctly, place the brooch pin in position in the hinge (joint) and push the hinge pin (wire) through so that the hinge is working. You will now find that the high inside edge of the hinge will not allow the brooch pin to meet the catch (Fig. 147). To remedy this and to give the pin correct spring, remove the hinge pin and brooch pin and, using a half round needle file, file the middle of the offending edge lower (Fig. 148). This should be done until, when the pin is in the hinge, it rests slightly above the catch (Fig. 149). In this way the pin will have a little upwards pressure when held in the catch and this will help keep it in position.

The correct length of the brooch pin can now be judged by placing it in position and cutting it 1/16″ from the outside of the catch. File a tapering point at the end so that it fits easily into the catch and does not have to be forced (Fig. 150).

To finish off the brooch, remove the pin and do any final polishing that is necessary. Then place the stone in position and hold the brooch firmly on your bench pin so that the fittings on the back do not become damaged.

Next, using the end of a ball pen or the end of a pencil, begin very gently to push each claw over the edge of the stone (Fig. 151). Bend the first claw, then the one diagonally opposite it, then the remaining two in the same way. Bend each claw a little at a time until the stone is held firmly. If when all claws are down on the stone it is still slightly loose, with great care, so as not to slip and crack the stone, use flat pliers gently to squeeze the claws slightly downwards, not on to the stone, but back towards their own bases (Fig. 152).

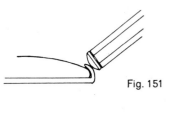
Fig. 151

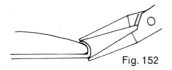
Fig. 152

When the setting of the stone is satisfactory, assemble the hinge and push the hinge pin through as far as it will go. Cut off each end, leaving 1/32″ showing (Fig. 153), and file them square, taking care not to scratch the brooch back.

Fig. 153

Finally, rivet each end so that the pin will not become loose. This is done with someone holding the brooch against the edge of your steel block, so that the end of the hinge pin rest on the top (Fig. 154). Then gently centre punch each end, slightly spreading the ends to make them larger and so stopping the pin from falling out (Fig. 155). The brooch is now finished and can be finally cleaned before wearing.

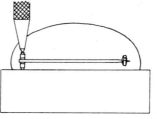
Fig. 154

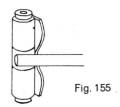
Fig. 155

Silver cufflinks

Cufflinks are always acceptable as presents, especially if you give a pair which have been specially made by you to suit the personality concerned. They can be inexpensive to give and, by using one of the suitable jeweller's findings, very easy to make. All you need basically is two small metal plates of your own design soldered on to the ready-made fittings which are readily available.

The pair in this exercise are very simple, but the instructions for them will apply to many alternative shapes that you may like to try later.

To make the round plates, scribe two circles with your dividers, each ⅝″ diameter, on to a suitable piece of flat sheet metal, gauge 18 or slightly thinner. Punch the centre of each circle lightly and, using a 1/16″ drill, drill half-way through the metal so that a shallow round indentation the width of the drill is left (Fig. 156). This will form the single decorative dot on the cufflinks, when finally filled with wax.

Next, check that these dots are still in the centre of your circles and if correct, cut the circles out with your piercing saw. True up the edges with a file and then smooth them with emery paper wrapped round a flat file.

To polish the front and back of these circles, first rub each side flat on a sheet of fine emery paper, and when all blemishes have been removed, use metal polish on a piece of leather to rub the surfaces until a bright polish is obtained.

When the plates are finished to this stage, next buy the fittings for the back of the cufflinks. The best type to buy is the one which has a separate hinge joint to solder on to the plates so that the main part can be riveted on after all the soldering is done (Fig. 157). This is necessary, because if the fitting is in one piece, when soldering is done the steel spring inside the sprung arm would be softened and become useless. However, if this type of fitting is not available, there are others which can be used. It is a good idea when buying one of these to ask the retailer to explain how they can be taken apart, because the spring arm must be removed for soldering and then assembled afterwards.

To attach the swivel type of fitting to your two plates, first flux the underneath of the two small hinge parts and, placing a little solder on each, hold them one at a time in the flame of your torch until the solder just runs. Next, flux the centre of the back of one of your plates, and place it on the asbestos sheet ready for soldering (Fig. 158). As in the previous piece, to aid heating the plate should be lifted slightly off the asbestos

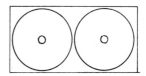

Fig. 156

Fig. 157

Fig. 158

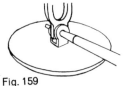

Fig. 159

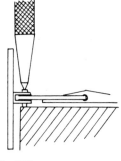

Fig. 160

by resting it on a couple of nails. Put the hinge piece in the centre in position and heat to allow the flux to settle. Re-position if necessary and heat the plate until the solder flows to form a good joint. Do the same to the remaining hinge, and repolish both to remove discolouration caused by heat.

All that remains to be done now is to assemble the links and plates together. When buying the fittings, you should have been given two small rivets to fit the holes in the hinge. If, however, they have been lost, two short lengths of 1/16" dia. wire can be used in place of them by filing one end of each into a long taper, thin enough to fit into the holes (Fig. 159).

If you have the proper rivets, they should be the correct size and length already. Therefore simply assemble the cufflinks and ask someone to hold each in turn on the edge of your steel block so that the head of the rivet rests firmly on the flat surface. You can then centre punch the other end of the rivet, so spreading it and holding it in place (Fig. 160).

However, if you are using wire in place of the rivets, push the tapered ends firmly into the holes and cut the excess wire each end off, leaving 1/32" showing either side of the hinges. Again ask someone to hold the cufflink on the edge of your steel block so that one end of the wire hinge pin rests firmly, and centre punch each end in turn. Be careful when doing this that no other parts become bent.

The cufflinks are now ready to wear except for filling the central dot on each face with wax so that it is more decorative. Special hard wax can be bought to do this, but any child's wax crayon will do. Simply rub it over the hole until it becomes filled then, to remove any excess, clean the surfaces with a clean rag and metal polish.

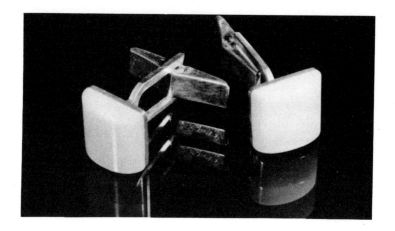

Ivory cufflinks

As an alternative to the plain silver cufflinks, these combine the use of another material with metal. The material used here is ivory, but there is no reason why another similar material such as one of the many different plastics or hard woods should not be used.

To make the basic metal parts of the cufflinks, cut two $\frac{1}{2}''$ squares of metal for the face plates, and except for omitting the decorative dot of the previous exercise, follow the same procedure until the metal parts are completed and polished except for the faces (Fig. 161).

When the cufflinks are at this stage, select a piece of ivory or other suitable material which you wish to use. If it is not already in a sheet, then saw it so that you have a piece large enough and approximately 3/16" thick. To ensure a good surface for glueing to the metal plate, rub one of the surfaces absolutely

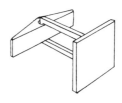

Fig. 161

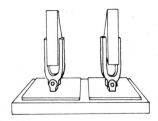

Fig. 162

Fig. 163

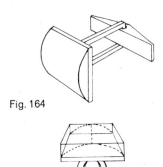

Fig. 164

Fig. 165

flat on a sheet of sandpaper.

Mix up sufficient epoxy glue on a clean surface, being careful to follow the maker's instructions, and spread a little evenly on the prepared surfaces. Place the metal plates in position on the sheet of material to be glued to them (Fig. 162), and press the surfaces firmly together. Avoid getting any glue on the polished backs, and if you do remove it straightaway with a moist rag.

Leave the cufflinks in this position for twenty-four hours, so that the glue hardens properly.

Then when dry, saw round the metal plates, being careful not to cut into the metal itself. Finish each edge off by filing the material level with the metal (Fig. 163).

The next stage is simply to round off each of the edges that will be top and bottom when worn in the cuff (Fig. 164). This is done by using a flat file to file an equal curve either side of a pencilled centre line (Fig. 165).

When this is done, smooth all the surfaces using fine emery paper wrapped round a file and carefully rounding any sharp edges.

Finally, when all marks have been removed, polish by using metal polish for ivory or plastic, or wax if you have used wood.

Earrings

Many attractive earrings can be made with beads. There is such a wealth of colour and shapes in the beads available that the variety is unlimited, and by using ready-made fittings the job of making is mostly done for you. In fact, it is largely only a question of assembling the beads and fittings together in a satisfactory way.

In this exercise, small square wooden beads of black and brown are used, but the method used to hang them can be easily adapted to suit any bead which has a hole drilled through it.

All that is needed to start is a piece of 1/16″ dia. wire 2½″ long. Straighten this in your fingers and, finding the middle, hold it in the wide part of the jaws of the round pliers and bend into a U shape as in Fig. 166.

Next, still using your round pliers, bend each side out slightly at a point ¼″ above the bottom curve (Fig. 167).

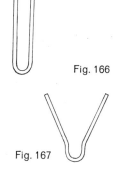

Fig. 166

Fig. 167

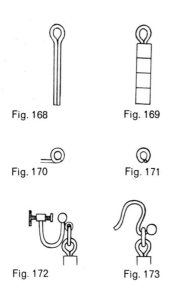

Fig. 168

Fig. 169

Fig. 170

Fig. 171

Fig. 172

Fig. 173

Hold the bottom curve in the middle of your pliers, and with your fingers push the two long sides together (Fig. 168).

This forms the wire on which the beads are to be threaded and glued. Now spread a little epoxy glue on the wire and on the inside of each bead. Thread four beads on to the two thicknesses of wire and line them up in their correct position. Cut off any excess wire sticking out of the bottom and leave to dry (Fig. 169).

The next part to make is the extra link which will allow the beads to hang freely. To make this, with the wide part of the jaws again make a loop in a short length of wire so that the end of the loop overlaps its beginning (Fig. 170).

Saw through the wire where the two thicknesses touch, so making a complete single ring, or jump ring as they are called, with one end slightly to the side of the other (Fig. 171).

Open this ring a little more by bending the ends sideways from each other, and thread it through the loop at the top of the bead wire. Close the gap in the ring by bending the two ends sideways together with flat pliers.

You are now ready to attach the beads to a suitable ear-ring fitting. The type used here is a screw fitting for un-pierced ears, and all that needs to be done is to thread the ring you have just made through the loop provided. This is done by opening the loop on the fitting carefully with round nosed pliers, putting the jump ring in place and closing the loop again so that the ring just remains free (Fig. 172).

If, however, you are making the earrings for pierced ears, you will need to buy ear wires instead of the screw fittings. These can then be attached to your jump ring by threading them through until the ball at the end of these wires stops the ring (Fig. 173).

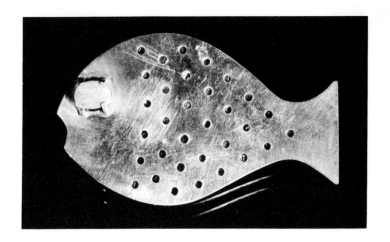

Fish brooch

To make this brooch, you will need a piece of flat sheet metal gauge 18 and approximately $2\frac{1}{2}''$ x $1\frac{1}{2}''$.

With a pencil and tracing paper, very carefully make a tracing of the drawing of the brooch as it is in Fig. 174 and transfer this to your metal sheet by the method described earlier on p. 42. When you are certain that a correct impression has been made on the surface of the metal, remove the tracing paper and scribe along the lines, also lightly centre punching each of the dots.

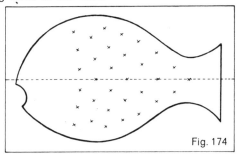

Fig. 174

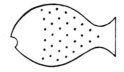 

Fig. 175

Cut out the shape of the fish by sawing just outside the line, and finish afterwards to its final shape by filing. When this is done, emery paper the edges smooth and rub the front and back surfaces flat on a sheet of fine emery so that the marks are removed and they are ready for final polishing.

Next, with a 1/16″ diameter drill, carefully half drill each of the dots that you have centre punched (Fig. 175). Try to keep each one as equally spaced as possible. Any burrs made by drilling can be removed by rubbing the front on the sheet of emery paper again. Polish all the surfaces by rubbing viorously with a soft piece of leather and metal polish until a bright even finish is obtained.

The setting of the stone comes next. In this piece the stone used is a small opal, but any small flat-backed stone of your choice may be used instead. The instructions for the setting should be followed and the actual size of your own stone substituted. When trying the stone in place, you will find that various expressions can be given to the character of the fish by slightly different positions. The choice of the actual position for the stone on the brooch, therefore, is really a matter of personal preference, and as long as it is not too near the edge any position similar to that illustrated can be used. When the stone is in a satisfactory position, stick a small piece of plasticine on the back of the stone to hold it in place on the brooch while you mark its shape with your scriber. The plasticine will hold it fairly still when it is pressed downwards into its correct place and so allow you lightly to scribe round the stone without fear of it moving. When you have marked out the shape, remove the stone and divide the circumference of the shape into four positions for the claws which will hold the stone. These should be evenly spaced around the shape of the stone so that it will be held properly and not fall out because of unduly large gaps between the claws (Fig. 176).

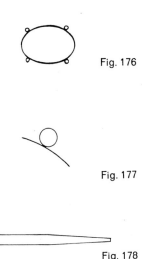

Fig. 176

Centre punch each of these places slightly outside the line marking the shape of the stone, so allowing for half the thickness of the wire to be used for the claw. The distance between the centre punch mark and the line should be 1/32".

Next, using a 1/16" drill, drill a hole at each of these claw positions so that when the stone is in place, the edge of the holes just touch the side of the stone (Fig. 177).

Fig. 177

To make the claws themselves, you will need four lengths of 1/16" round wire each ½" long. However, before you cut these lengths, they will be easier to hold if you file a long taper (Fig. 178) to fit the holes, using a long length each time, then cutting them to the right length afterwards. The tapers on the wires should push through the holes so that a little protrudes at the back of the brooch (Fig. 179).

Fig. 178

Fig. 179

It will make soldering easier if, when in position, all the claws stand exactly the same height, so try them and trim a little off any which are too long (Fig. 180).

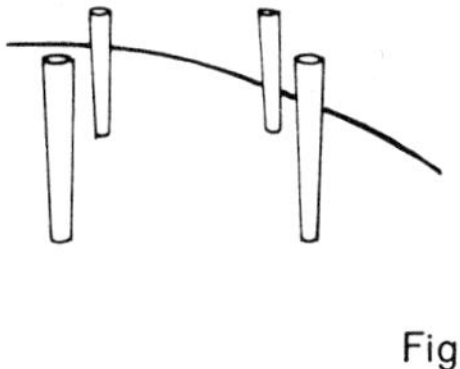

To solder the claws, first push them firmly into place and flux them front and back. Stand the brooch face downwards on

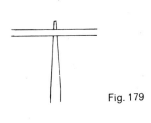

Fig. 180

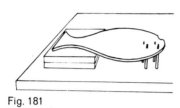

Fig. 181

Fig. 182

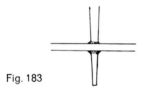

Fig. 183

Fig. 184

the asbestos, so that it stands squarely on the ends of all four claws. To do this you will need to use something the right height to prop up the rear end of the fish (Fig. 181). A few small pieces of asbestos sheet will do, and these can be cut from the corner of your sheet. When the brooch is properly in position, heat until the flux settles, then place four small pieces of lead solder against the ends of the claws where they protrude through (Fig. 182).

Reheat, playing the flame of your torch evenly on the area around the claws until the solder flows. Allow to cool then turn over the brooch to see whether the solder has also run through the hole and round the bottom of each claw on the front of the brooch (Fig. 183). If not, put the brooch back into its former position and reheat so that the solder flows again. Do not overheat, however, as the solder may run on to your polished surfaces, so spoiling them.

When the soldering is satisfactory, wash off the flux and dry. Then, with end cutters, cut off the bits of the claw where they protrude through the back of the brooch. Rub the back surface on emery paper to remove all excess solder and any scratches (Fig. 184). Finally, polish with a piece of leather and metal polish.

Try the stone in your setting
but do not force it in. If the
stone does not fit, then using
a needle file very carefully
so as not to scratch the
polished surfaces, file a little
off the inside of each claw until
the stone sits flat (Fig. 185).
When the stone is sitting
correctly, judge how long the
claws will need to be to bend
over the edges of the stone, as
in Fig. 186, and cut them to
that length. Finally, so that the
claws will bend easily on to
the stone when it is set into the
brooch, remove the stone and
file each claw into a wedge
shape (Fig. 187). Be careful
not to mark the surrounding
surface while doing this.

Fig. 185

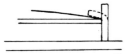

Fig. 186

When the setting is finished
to this stage, the next step is to
solder the catch and pin on to
the back of the brooch. This is
done in exactly the same way
as the procedure given on p.
62. The hinge part (joint) of
the catch should be soldered
about $\frac{1}{4}''$ in from the edge and
the pin fitted to the correct
length (Fig. 188). The only
difference is that when setting
up the brooch on the asbestos
for soldering, the claws should
be resting squarely on the ·
asbestos. This is because if the
solder holding them in does
melt whilst soldering on the
catch, the claws will be held
in by their taper fit and the
weight of the brooch. However,
try to avoid soldering the

Fig. 187

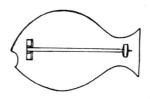

Fig. 188

77

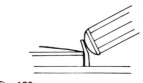

Fig. 189

Fig. 190

catch too near to the back of the claws and so having to heat where they are.

When the catch is complete, the next job is to set the stone into the brooch. To do this, first place the stone into position and hold the brooch firmly in your bench pin so that the catch on the back is in the V opening. Then, using a small piece of hard wood or the round end of a plastic ball pen, begin to push each of the claws over the edge of the stone (Fig. 189). Bend each claw in turn a little at a time, working on pairs diagonally across the stone until all are down as far as they will go, so holding the stone firmly in place (Fig. 190).

Finally, before the brooch is complete, all the dots on the body of the fish should be filled with black wax. This is done by using a child's wax crayon and rubbing it evenly over the dotted surface until all the dots are filled. Any excess can then be removed with metal polish, and the brooch cleaned ready for wearing.

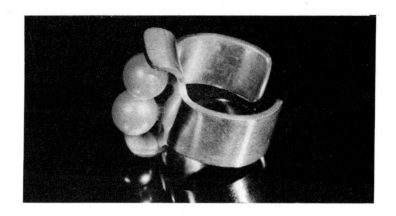

Pearl ring

It is usual when making a ring by hand to make it so that it will fit the finger of the person concerned exactly. However, to provide individual fitting entails more complicated methods and tools than is generally practical in the home, and so the rings in this and the following exercise have a split shank or finger band. This allows the ring to be adjusted to fit any finger, and all that is necessary to obtain the various fittings is to bend carefully the finger band so that the two ends become nearer or wider apart, so changing the diameter size of the ring.

The stones used in the ring in this exercise are two imitation pearls with holes drilled in one side of them so that they can be glued on to a suitable peg on the ring. These pearls are sold already drilled and can often be bought very cheaply from local craft shops or from some of the retailers listed at the back of the book. The size of the pearls that you will require are $\frac{1}{4}''$ diameter.

The metal needed to make this ring is a rectangle of flat sheet, $2'' \times 1\frac{1}{8}''$. On to this, mark out the shape of the ring as it is shown in Fig. 191, and cut it out with your piercing saw. File the edges to their final shape and smooth them with fine emery paper. When this is done, carefully mark out the positions for the two small pegs on to which the pearls will be glued. These should be $\frac{1}{4}''$ apart, so that when the

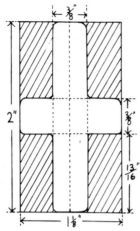

Fig. 191

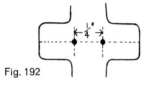

Fig. 192

Fig. 193

Fig. 194

pearls are in place they just touch each other. Centre punch each mark lightly, then drill both holes with a 1/32″ drill (Fig. 192).

Before going further, it is best to remove now any scratches etc. from the surfaces of your ring with fine emery paper and to polish it, because this will be more difficult later.

Next, as a guide to bending up the two protective ends of the setting, draw a line across in pencil $\frac{1}{8}$″ from each end. Hold the metal in the flat pliers so that the inner edge of the jaws comes along this line and is parallel to the edges of the finger band (Fig. 193). Now holding the metal firmly, bend each end upwards until they are at right angles. Try to keep this so that the ends stand up at equal heights (Fig. 194). However, if they do vary slightly, carefully file a little off the offending one until they are the same.

To bend the band of the ring to fit your finger, you will need an object around which to mallet it to shape. Any metal or wooden rod that is approximately $\frac{5}{8}$″ in diameter can be used, as long as it has a smooth surface. A short length of hard wood rod such as dowelling can be bought quite cheaply from a local supplier and this will be ideal.

Use your G clamp to hold

this rod on to your working top so that a few inches protrude over the edge. This will hold it steady while you mallet the ring round it (Fig. 195).

When bending the ring, start at each end and work towards the middle, gently malleting each end in turn until the band becomes circular (Fig. 196). Do not attempt to mallet the setting, as this will only damage its shape. If after bending the ring round the rod it is still too large for your finger, hold each side of the band in turn on your bench top and very gently mallet the ring into a tighter circle, turning the ring round as you go (Fig. 197).

When it is a good fit, repolish the ring, paying special attention to the space where the pearls will sit because you will be unable to polish this later when the ring is complete.

To make the pegs which will hold the pearls, file two $\frac{1}{2}''$ lengths of 1/16" diameter wire into long tapers, so that one end of each goes through the back of the holes drilled in the ring and projects $\frac{1}{8}''$ into the place where the pearls will be (Fig. 198). When they are in position, make certain that the projecting piece of this taper will fit snugly into the holes of the pearls without forcing them on (Fig. 199).

In order to avoid unnecessary solder spoiling the front surface of the setting, the soldering

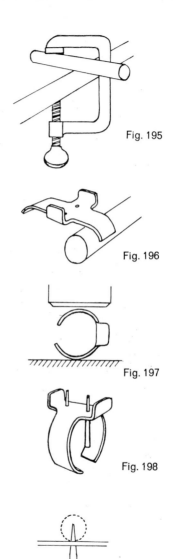

Fig. 195

Fig. 196

Fig. 197

Fig. 198

Fig. 199

of these pegs is done from the back, as with the claws in the previous piece. Place the peg in position, leaving the excess length of the peg sticking out into the inside of the ring. Flux both front and back and stand the ring upside down so that it rests on the two ends of the setting on the asbestos sheet (Fig. 200). Solder it by placing a little lead solder against the back of each peg, and heat it equally so that it flows around the peg on both sides. When this is done, cut off the excess length of wire at the back of the setting and file it flush with the surface. Then remove any file marks and scratches with emery paper (Fig. 201).

Re-polish the ring with metal polish to remove any discolouration from soldering, and carefully scrape clean the two pegs so that all is ready for glueing on the pearls. Finally, mix up a little epoxy glue on a clean surface and with a match stick spread some evenly along each peg. Push the pearls firmly into place (Fig. 202), and leave for twenty-four hours so that the glue sets firm before you wear the ring.

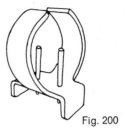

Fig. 200

Fig. 201

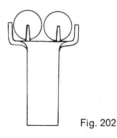

Fig. 202

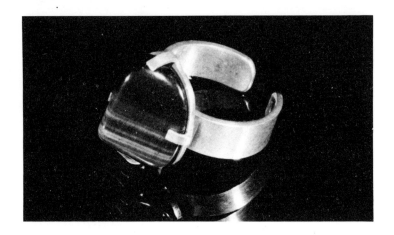

Ring

This second ring is of a very simple straightforward design and the instructions for making it can easily be applied to any fairly large, flat-backed, opaque stone. It is composed of two pieces, the open band which can be adjusted to fit any finger and a simple setting of the type used in the first brooch exercise. There is, therefore, no reason why a number of such rings should not be made, using basically the same type of mount but with various stones that interest you.

In this way you can easily make a whole series of rings to suit various clothes.

To make the first part of the ring, which is the open band to go round the finger, simply cut a rectangle of sheet metal 2″ x ¾″. File it true, polish it and bend into a circle to fit your finger as with the previous ring (Fig. 196).

When this band is finished, to make the next piece, which is the setting, place your stone

Fig. 203

on a suitable piece of metal sheet and scribe carefully round it. Mark on four claws of a suitable length to hold your stone in place (Fig. 204). Cut out the shape, file it, emery the edges and polish the back surface. Bend all the claws up at right angles as near to the edge as possible and file them to their correct tapers.

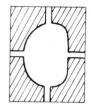

Fig. 204

Next, to solder the ring and the setting together, first place the setting upside down on your asbestos sheet, so that it rests on the end of its four claws. Paint a little flux in the middle area of the back of the setting and on the band, directly opposite the open ends. Place the band in position on the setting so that it rests centrally with its end at the top (Fig. 205).

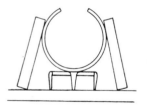

Fig. 205

To keep it in the correct position, you may need to prop it in place from either side with two small pieces of asbestos (Fig. 206). Solder it by placing a small piece of lead solder either side of the intended joint (Fig. 207), and equally heat the two pieces until the solder flows between the ring and the setting. Allow the joint to cool, wash off flux, and re-polish the ring to remove any stains. The final step is setting the stone into your ring, and this should be done as described at the end of the exercise on the first simple brooch.

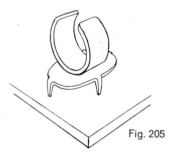

Fig. 206

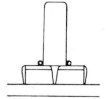

Fig. 207

If the stone that you wish to use is a mineral sample, as here, and therefore of a slightly uneven shape, it is advisable when setting to use a little epoxy glue to help hold the stone firmly in place. This should be spread on the back of the stone and on the face of the setting before the claws are finally pushed firmly over the edge of the stone. If, however, a properly cut stone is to be used, this is not necessary and the claws will be sufficient for normal wear and tear.

Perspex (Plexiglas) and metal pendant

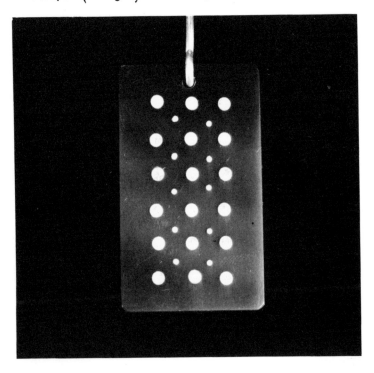

In almost every different type of article of jewelry, the combination of another material with metal can provide interesting variations. This is true both when the material is used either as a stone would be, mounted into your jewelry, or where it forms the major part of the article with metal becoming secondary. The ivory cufflinks previously made can be said to belong to the first category, and the pendant we are about to make is an example of the second. Here the material used provides the main area of the piece and the metal studs become the decorative quality.

The material used for this piece is blue Perspex or Plexigas, but any suitable hard piece of wood, ivory or other material can be substituted. Also, if you wish, the actual shape of the pendant can be varied slightly to suit your own taste, or extended into a number of matching pieces of jewelry.

When you have decided what material to use, the first job is to saw and file it into a rectangle 1¾″ long and 1″ wide and ⅛″ to ¼″ thick. This must be well done with all the corners square and all the surfaces rubbed flat on a sheet of fine emery cloth. If Perspex sheet is to be used, then all you need do is simply saw out the rectangle from a suitable piece of ⅛″ or ¼″ thickness, which can be bought at a local supplier.

When you have your rectangle of Perspex or other material ready, lightly scribe out the grid of guide lines ⅛″ apart as shown in Fig. 208.

To obtain variety in the size of the metal dots in the finished pendant, you will need two different thicknesses of wire, one 1/16″ and one 1/32″ in diameter. This change of size, however, is not absolutely necessary and all one size can be used throughout if preferred. If this is the case, then all holes should be drilled the same diameter. Using your grid of lines, mark a small indentation with the point of

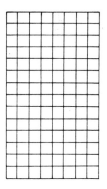

Fig. 208

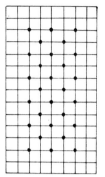

Fig. 209

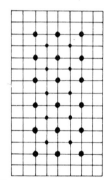

Fig. 210

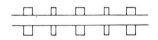

Fig. 211

your scriber at the appropriate junctions of the lines as a starting guide for your drill (Fig. 209).

Holding your drill at 90° to the surface of your material, carefully drill each point with a 1/32" drill, trying to keep all holes evenly spaced apart. When this is completed satisfactorily, change your drill for one of 1/16" diameter, and redrill those holes shown in Fig. 210.

Next, cut short lengths of wire to fit these holes so that a little sticks out on either side (Fig. 211). You may find that the burrs left on the ends through cutting with your wire cutters will need to be removed with a fine file before the wire will fit into the hole.

Mix up a little epoxy glue and with a spare piece of wire poke some into each hole. Then, one at a time, spread a little along each wire and push them into place. Try to ensure a good joint each time by using sufficient glue and do not worry if some of the glue spreads on to the surface of your material, because this will be removed later when the faces are filed down flat. When all the wires are glued into position, leave the glue to harden for twenty-four hours before disturbing.

Before continuing, make sure that the glue has set hard and that all the wires are held firmly

in place. If there are any
which move, these must be
taken out, cleaned, re-glued
and left for a further twenty-four
hours.

Fig. 212

When all the wires are
properly glued, with a flat file
and working across the whole
of each surface in turn, file the
wires down until they are
almost flush with the surface
of your material (Fig. 212).
Next, continue by rubbing the
two surfaces down on a medium
grade of emery paper until
they are absolutely flat, with
all wires flush and any
scratches or excess glue
removed. Next, to finish the
surfaces, smooth them and the
edges by rubbing on a finer
grade of emery paper and then
polish them with leather and
metal polish until a good finish
is obtained. Except for the
hole for the link which hangs
the pendant from the chain, the
main part of the pendant is
now complete. This hole should
be carefully drilled with a 3/32"
drill, and placed in the centre
$\frac{1}{8}''$ down from the top edge
(Fig. 213).

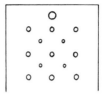

Fig. 213

Fig. 214

To make the connecting link,
cut a piece of 1/16" diameter
wire $1\frac{3}{4}''$ in length, and using
the widest part of the jaws
of the round nosed pliers make
a cranked loop at each end
so that they line up (Fig. 214).
Open one of these loops slightly
and thread it through the
pendant (Fig. 215). Then close

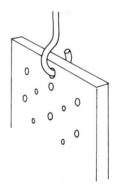

Fig. 215

Fig. 216

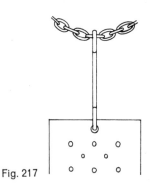

Fig. 217

Fig. 218

Fig. 219

it with the flat pliers, taking care not to mark the polished surfaces of the pendant.

All that remains now is to buy the length of chain that you need to fit your neck and a suitable bolt (spring) ring together with two jump rings (Fig. 216). The chain should be slightly under $\frac{1}{8}''$ in width so that it will fit through the loop in your link. The actual length of the chain should be approximately 2′, though this length can be varied slightly according to where you wish the pendant to hang. Chain made from different metals can be bought from various sources, but if you have any trouble, it can generally be obtained from the retailers of jeweller's findings listed on p. 95. The bolt (spring) ring and the two jump rings can also be bought from these retailers, and the size that you need is $\frac{1}{4}''$ diameter (Fig. 216). Thread the chain through the top loop of your link (Fig. 217), and at each end put a jump ring. This is done by bending the ring with flat pliers so that the ends move apart sideways, enabling you to thread them on to the chain (Fig. 218). On to one of these jump rings add the side loop of your bolt ring. Close each of these jump rings by bending the ends sideways towards each other until they touch (Fig. 219), making a complete ring without a gap.

As an alternative to using a chain on which to hang your pendant, a narrow leather thong can be used as an attractive substitute. Good quality long leather bootlaces make ideal thongs. To attach the thong to your pendant pass it through the loop on the pendant link. Then make the ends so that they can be clipped together properly by threading a jump ring on at one end so that about $\frac{1}{2}''$ of the thong shows through. Fold this end back to touch the rest of the thong and, putting a little glue on the inside surfaces, hold them together and wind a suitable length of cotton evenly and tightly round the two thicknesses, so making it a neat join (Fig. 220). At the other end of your thong thread the loop of the bolt ring and again glue and bind the two ends together into a neat joint (Fig. 221).

Fig. 220

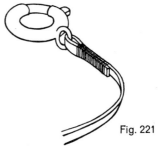

Fig. 221

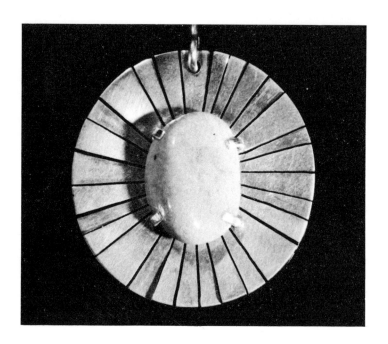

Pendant

As a central area of colour in this pendant a polished pink mineral sample has been used. This stone is a piece of Rhodochrosite, but any flat backed stone of your own choice may be used instead and the instructions given for setting the stone adapted to suit.

· To make the main part of this pendant, you will first need a square of flat sheet metal 1⅛″ x 1¾″ and approximately gauge 18 in thickness. Find the centre of this piece of metal, lightly centre punch it and then with dividers describe a circle of 1¾″ in diameter (Fig. 222). When this is done, cut the circle out with your saw and file the edge true.

As it will be very difficult to polish the shape properly at a later stage, all surfaces should now be smoothed with fine emery paper and polished with leather and metal polish. Do not, however, remove the centre mark entirely, as you will need this later.

When polishing is complete, stick a little piece of plasticine on the back of your stone and position the stone in the centre of your circle. As a helpful guide, use a pair of pencil compasses to draw a circle slightly bigger than your stone, so that you can judge better when the stone is in the right place (Fig. 223). When you are satisfied that it is, very carefully scribe round the shape of the stone, making sure it does not move from its position.

Remove the stone and mark out four equally spaced positions around the shape of the stone where the claws will be soldered. Remember that these must be so placed round the stone that they will stop it from moving or falling out, and that they should also be evenly balanced when the pendant is being worn. Next, allowing for half the thickness of the wire which will be used for the claws, centre punch and drill each position with a 1/16″ drill, so that the edge of the hole just touches the line marking the shape of the stone (Fig. 224). Cut four $\frac{1}{2}$″ lengths of 1/16″ diameter wire for the claws, and fit each of these through the holes that you have drilled so that about $\frac{1}{8}$″ protrudes at the back of the pendant (Fig. 225). Flux both the front and back of each joint and place the

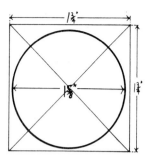

Fig. 222

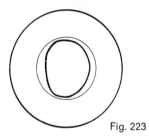

Fig. 223

Fig. 224

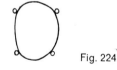

Fig. 225

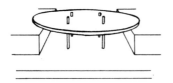

Fig. 226

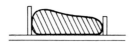

Fig. 227

pendant upside down on your asbestos so that it rests evenly on the ends of the four claws. If the wires are loose in their holes and keep slipping through, place some small pieces of asbestos under either side of the pendant to hold it approximately ⅛" up from the sheet (Fig. 226). Place a little bit of lead solder against the wire where it protrudes through the back, and solder each one in turn making sure that the solder flows to both front and back of the joint. Wash off the flux and file flat any excess solder or claw sticking out at the back. Finally rub on a sheet of fine emery to remove any file marks before re-polishing the back and the front if necessary.

Try the fit of your stone and if any of the claws stop it from sitting down flat, carefully file a little off the inside of the offending claws until it does fit properly. Then, with the stone in position, judge the length of the claws required to bend over the end of the stone properly and cut them to their correct length. This will normally be the same for all four claws, but if an uneven shaped stone is being used, it may be necessary to vary them slightly in order to make them hold the stone firm (Fig. 227). When the claws are cut correctly, carefully file each one into a taper as described previously so that they will bend easily over the stone when it is set into your pendant.

The next stage is to mark out the radiating lines to be cut into the pendant (Fig. 228). These can be drawn to your own choice, but each line should radiate from the centre mark and be slightly differently spaced so that the segments left vary in width. Do not make them any thinner than ⅛" at their widest part, however, as this will make them too narrow and weak in the middle of your pendant. Also, do allow sufficient metal either side of the claws, and leave one segment at the top of the pendant a ¼" wide so that it can be drilled to take a connecting link and make the pendant hang properly. Each line should finish where it touches the shape of the stone already marked.

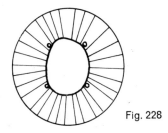

Fig. 228

Having marked the lines out satisfactorily, use your piercing saw to cut carefully along each line, trying to keep the cuts as straight as possible because no filing can be done to the edges to straighten them up. When all the cutting is finished, place your stone in its setting and push all the claws firmly over the edge of the stone with a suitable plastic or hard wood tool so that it is held firmly in position (Fig. 229). Next, $\frac{1}{8}''$ down from the top of the wide segment from which the pendant will be suspended, lightly centre punch and drill a central hole 1/16" diameter (Fig. 230).

Fig. 229

The final thing to be done to this part of the pendant is gently to bend the segments to slightly varying heights so that the pendant is given an undulating surface to add interest. This is done by simply pushing each segment to a position slightly higher or lower than its neighbour with a small piece of wood filed to a round point (Fig. 231). Do not bend them too much, however; generally the thickness of the metal up or down is sufficient movement.

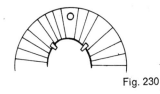

Fig. 230

The main part of the pendant is now complete, and the next

Fig. 231

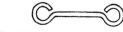

Fig. 232

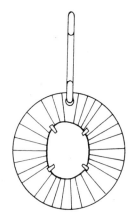

Fig. 233

piece to make is the connecting link from which it will hang. For this, cut a length of 1/16" diameter wire 2" long and at each end make a cranked loop using the widest part of the jaws of your round nosed pliers (Fig. 232). Open one loop slightly and thread it through the hole in your pendant. Then close with flat pliers so that the pendant hangs from the link freely (Fig. 234).

Finally, to finish your pendant, you will need to buy a suitable length of chain, two jump rings and a bolt (spring) ring. The actual length of the chain should be approximately 2', though this can be varied according to your choice of position for the pendant to hang. The chain should be assembled as described at the end of the previous pendant, or if preferred, a leather thong can be substituted.

Why not make more jewelry?

In conclusion, I hope that you have discovered in jewelry-making a pastime which has proved both interesting and enjoyable. If this is the case, it is possible that you would like to pursue it further, and a good way to follow up your knowledge is to join a jewelry-making class. Many education authorities run beginners classes for evening students, and you will find the atmosphere of working with other interested people of great benefit.

If, however, it is impossible to attend such a class, why not study on at home? If you have carefully followed all the exercises in this book, you will already have not only sufficient experience and tools to continue on your own at home, but also a good basis on which to learn the more advanced methods that can be used. You can extend your knowledge with the help of some of the books listed below.

As some immediate help, a selection of jewellery not included in the exercises is shown in the colour plate facing p. 81. These pieces, though generally more complicated than the jewelry you have been making, will serve perhaps to give you some ideas.

For further reading

Handwrought Jewelry by Lois Franke. McKnight, Illinois.
How To Make Modern Jewelry by the Museum of Modern Art. Simon & Schuster, New York.
Jewelry and Enameling by Greta Pack. Van Nostrand, New York.
Jewelry Making for the Amateur by Klares Lewes. Batsford, London. Reinhold, New York.
Make Your Own Costume Jewelry by Jutta Lammer. Batsford, London. Watson-Guptill, New York.

List of suppliers

Jeweller's findings and tools:
    E. Gray & Son Ltd, 12 Clerkenwell Rd, London, E.C.1.
    S. Lanzetter, 36 New Brown St, Manchester 4.
    J. F. Simmett, 39 Hope St, Glasgow, C.2.
    Charles Cooper Ltd, 92 Hatton Garden, London, E.C.1. and 83 Gt Hampton St, Birmingham 18.
    Herring, Morgan & Southon Ltd, 9 Berwick St, London, W.1.
    Allcraft, 15 West 45th St, New York, N.Y. 10036.
    American Handicraft Co., Inc., 20 West 14th St, New York.
    Anchor Tool & Supply Co., Inc., 12 John St, New York, N.Y. 10038.
Silver wire and sheet:
    Engelhard Industries Ltd, 52 High Holborn, London W.C.1. and 123 Vyse St, Birmingham 18.
    E. Gray & Son Ltd (see above).
    Johnson Matthey & Co. Ltd, 73 Hatton Garden, London, E.C.1.
    T. B. Hagstoz & Son, Metal Craft Department, Philadelphia 6, Pa.

Copper sheet:

    London Metal Warehouses Ltd, 15 Edgware Rd, London, W.C.2.; 269 Molesey St, Birmingham; Stanley Rd, Stockport and 25 Castlewood, Newcastle.

    T. B. Hagstoz & Son (see above).

Stones

    E. H. Dobbins & Co. Ltd, 3 Holborn Circus, London, E.C.1.

    Frank E. King, 10 Albermarle Way, Clerkenwell, London, E.C.1.

    Laurier Jewellery Ltd, 16 Greville St, London, E.C.1.

    A. Sechaud & Co. Ltd, 175 Piccadilly, London, W.1.

    Bernard C. Lowe & Co. Ltd, 4 Northampton St, Birmingham.

    Gemstones Ltd, 23 Hatton Garden, London, E.C.1.

    Nathan Gem & Pearl Co., Inc., 580 Fifth Avenue, New York, N.Y. 10036.

    International Gem Corp., 15 Maiden Lane, New York, N.Y. 10038.

    Astro Mineral Ltd, 511 West 33rd St, New York.

Index